Welcome to the first Publication fo
CHURCH OF GOD ON EARTH (COG

INSPIRED MESSAGES

This small Booklet contains Medium Messages from some well known Biblical Characters, who work on our behalf still, to help to save the EARTH, for the benefit of our World, our Race, and other Species, now and in the Future.

'INSPIRED MESSAGES' is extracted from the 'BOOK OF TRUTH AND KNOWLEDGE', this publication has so far been rejected by 22 Publishers in the UK, but it is now available to be ordered, together with some Merchandise, to be used for Advertising and Fund-Raising, at the new WEB-SITE, where you can learn further about the intentions for the Future.

WEB-SITE   www.cogoe.org.uk.

Thank you for your support, please help by telling your friends, by buying the Book, and by using the Merchandise. A Charity status has been applied for. A new platform to reach everyone who will listen is to be established. Healing is to be offered. We will move forwards as resources of people and finance become available.
May GOD bless you.

1. INSPIRED MESSAGES available now from 02.02.02
2. SPIRITUAL DEVELOPMENT .....available from 04.04.02
3. BOOK OF TRUTH and KNOWLEDGE available from 05.06.02

Books 2 and 3 can be pre-ordered at discount now by using the Web Site.

JOHN

PREFACE

Many SOULS have contributed to this Book, many SOULS have contributed to my LIFE, and many SOULS deserve to be thanked for their sacrifice, for their time and for their contributions. We are never alone, we think that we are, but we are led, we are guided, we are supported, we are directed, yes sometimes we are even pushed, if that is what is necessary for us to grasp the Opportunity or to learn the Lesson which is presented to us.

I feel very humble, for without the Input from ALL those about me, All those in my Peer- Group, yes even those who have brought to me the hard lessons of Rejection! it would not have been possible for me to be here today, in this Lifetime, writing this Book.
A huge thank you therefore to ALL those on the Earth-Plane who have enriched my Life; I ask for your indulgence and your forgiveness for any unhappiness which I have brought into your Life, both this One and the many previous Encounters. I hope and pray that we BOTH have learnt and progressed from the Relationships and will continue to do so.
I wish to include here my Family, Friends, Acquaintances, Colleagues, Girlfriends, Lovers, Wives, Children, and in particular those who are identified in this Book. I hope that you will be sympathetic to my reasons for recording our experiences, and will not feel too offended by me making this Public knowledge.
A particular big thank you to the Heavenly Father for this opportunity and the Trust given to me, to my Guides and to High Spirit, for their unceasing, tireless efforts, and to those Souls who have gone before and have chosen to return to help me. (I.e. Ted, Emma, Gertie, Alice and other family members from previous generations.)

- <u>The purpose of this Book</u> is to help Others to follow, to hopefully gain the Understanding, and so to bring LOVE, Compassion and Understanding into their own Lives and into the Lives of everyone they meet and every LIFE-FORM they have contact with.

- <u>The purpose of this Book</u> is to help YOU to progress towards the LIGHT, so that we ALL have a Future on this Planet, Earth, and that Future is built upon mutual Respect, Caring, Sharing and Understanding of the Roles we all play, so that the lessons can be learned in Peace and Harmony if at all possible.

• _The purpose of this Book_ is to help to prepare a platform of Understanding, to prepare the World for the coming of the New MESSIAH.

• _The purpose of this Book_ is to raise Funds, so as to support the Work of the new CHURCH of GOD on EARTH, and to publicize its Existence.

• _The purpose of this Book_ is to provide Guidance, Teaching and Assistance to Any who wish <u>to promote LOVE, to find their SOUL within, to help to Save the Planet for future Generations, to help to bring about Heaven on Earth.</u>

• _The purpose of this Book_ is to enlighten the understanding of Many associated with the man-made Religions throughout the World.

I am not saying that much of what is done in the name of GOD is incorrect. ANY Action or Belief, which supports GOD and which teaches LOVE, Harmony, Peace, Compassion, Sharing, Caring, and Tolerance to Others, is to be praised and to be supported.
Let no one be BIGOTED, Let no one believe that 'they' are greater than Another, Let no one cause Suffering to Others and hide behind a Religious Banner.

JOHN OLIVER NEWARK
See Web Site... **www.cogoe.org.uk.**

Copyright © 2,001 John Oliver Newark

All rights reserved. No part of this publication may be reproduced or transmitted in any form, or by any means electronic or mechanical, including photocopy, recording or any information retrieval system, without permission in writing from the Author. To include all International Conventions and Worldwide rights.

Published by: BADGER INVESTMENTS
PO BOX 119
BICESTER DO
OX26 4WD
UK
Printed by: Antony Rowe LTD
CHIPPENHAM
WILTS. UK
SN14 6LH

First Edition February 2002   ISBN 0-9542060-0-2

INTRODUCTION

1.00 This Book has been written at the instigation of High Spirit who work tirelessly on behalf of the One Supreme Power (GOD) to bring Enlightenment, Peace, Love and Harmony to every Life-form in our World and also to those Life-forms who exist throughout the Universe.

1.01 The purpose for the Book is to help to prepare those who are willing to listen, in readiness for the New Millennium. It is necessary for the World to change, so that all Lifeforms have the opportunity to survive. Without a significant movement towards Light, Love and Goodness there can be no doubt that the Human Race as we know it today, will not survive.

1.02 The question is, if you were GOD, what would you do to change peoples Attitudes, the way in which they relate to each other and also to the rest of God's Creation?
Evil continues to take an upper-hand; week-after-week and month-after-month we learn of Genocide, Slavery, Poverty, Greed, Wars and Atrocities, we learn of Rain Forest devastation, we learn of Genetically Modified Foods, we learn of Aids and Ozone holes in the Atmosphere, 150,000 Abortions in 1997 in the UK alone. Mankind is destroying the Balance of Nature.

1.03 The difficulty is the Free Will, which has been granted to Mankind. Let no-one doubt that what has been given can also be removed. GOD has used Floods, Plagues, Nature, to wipeout Mankind and to enable Man to start again viz. Noah, Atlantis. GOD has sent Jesus, Buddha, Mohammed, and other Prophets to tell us how to Act, how to treat our Neighbors and indeed to warn us that unless we change our Actions that the Wrath of GOD will descend. Alas, nothing so far has had a lasting effect.

1.04 Into this situation a New Measure is to be introduced. The Human Race is to be brought to a new level of Spiritual Awareness, so that we can receive immediate Communication with Spirit and GOD. It is believed that if Humans understand the 'raison d'être' for all their Actions, then there is the hope that correct Choices can be made; Guidance can be given and ALL can move towards the Light and Goodness of GOD.

1.05 The World is to be prepared for the coming of the new Messiah.
KEYPOINT INT1 :
Question every Meeting, every Event, every Action, it all has a Purpose, there is no such thing as pure Coincidence.

1.06 The name of this Book, the timing of this Book, the name of the New Church and the Words within this Book have all been supplied by High Spirit and transcribed by me and by other Mediums. In the same way the Bible was written; Humans were instrumental in recording their Observations and writing down the Words of Jesus. Jesus was perhaps the greatest Spiritual Medium who has ever walked the Earth-Plane. He was a Human Being, with a wonderful ancient Spirit, who chose to sacrifice himself, so that the Human Race could learn and be made aware of the Love of GOD, the survival of the Spirit, and the manner in which we should love and behave to each Other.

1.07 Jesus was a man who was declared by High Spirit as a Son of GOD, he was given the Holy Ghost (Holy Spirit, Solar Force, Christ Spirit, etc) and a significant sector of his Spirit was that of GOD. <u>YOU too can also aspire to become a Son or Daughter of God</u> by Giving your Life to GOD, by carrying out his Works and by achieving the necessary Awareness so that You the Mind Being, can be at one with your Soul and can communicate with High Spirit. We all have in the Spirit, a part of GOD, some, have more than Others.
KEYPOINT INT2
Jesus was a Man. Jesus became a Son of GOD through his Choices and Actions. You can also follow in his Footsteps. High Spirit can choose to appoint you as a Son or Daughter of GOD, should this be appropriate for you.

1.08 Many will consider the Book of Truth and Knowledge as fiction, their Minds will dismiss some or all of what is given. However, their Spirits will remember and when they return to the Earth-Plane, as they must eventually, then their learning and understanding will be that more advanced, which will enable them to progress their Understanding. If they learn but one KEYPOINT then this Book will have been worthwhile.

1.09 For those of you who do Believe and for those of you who wish to Embrace and Explore and Find out for themselves about their Destinies, then I hope that this Book will cause you to Question every Meeting, every Event and every Action which you take, and which happens to you. I hope that you will choose to search for your <u>Spiritual Awareness</u>, that you will choose to Respect every Creation of Nature and GOD, that you will choose to Treat every Person as you yourself would wish to be Treated.

1.10 And if you have the Abilities, the Time and the Opportunity, then I ask that you spread the word to Others and join or participate in the local activities of a Spiritual Group. <u>It is important that your Objective is not only to progress your own personal Awareness, but also to help Others and so to lighten the total Environment and so to participate in the ultimate Goal of achievement of Heaven On Earth.</u>

KEYPOINT INT3
HEAVEN will be achieved on the Earth-Plane, when a critical number of Souls are Enlightened. At this Time the Future of this Planet will be assured, and the Human Race will have Earned the right to remain here. At the present Time the Human Race is on Trial and the Planet is only loaned to us.

1.11 I reiterate, at risk is the survival of everything we know of in our present World. What I ask is the point of accumulating Wealth and building a World based on the misery and suffering of Others, for that World to be destroyed by Others or by Nature or by GOD.

1.12 I have used only Forenames in order to protect those who do not wish to be identified. I have also changed all of those Forenames in order to avoid the threatened litigation by some. I also wish to protect those People who are still alive and do not wish to have publicity. I apologize to anyone who may feel offended by my words, this was never my intention.

1.13 I appreciate that many People are set in their ways, are devoted to their own beliefs and are committed to existing Churches. I would only ask them to read my words and then to consider in their own Hearts what is correct. There are many Books and many Religions, not all are incorrect, there are many good People about, there are many correct concepts, and much can be learned from the Ancients and from our Ancestors. However:
What is completely wrong is Mankind's Intolerance and Mankind's Bigotry to Others.
What is completely wrong is the sinful way in which Religious Zealots practice Hypocrisy and believe that their Way is exclusive, to the exclusion of Others, Beliefs.
What is unacceptable is that UNLESS Mankind changes its ATTITUDES and BEHAVIOUR, then ALL will FAIL. THERE IS NO CHOICE, WE HAVE TO CHANGE.

1.14 We, All, can choose to <u>PRAY to the one GOD</u>, or to JESUS, or through your own PROPHET to the one GOD. We, All, can choose to Walk in the Footsteps of Jesus.

1.15 The New Testament was written some 2,000 years ago in a language intended to be understood by Peoples living at that Time. Nothing stands still, if it does it dies, it becomes a Relic to be interpreted and to be misunderstood. There are many good and wonderful Words written in the Testaments, many apply today, however some Religious Groups interpret the Words to suit their own Understanding. There are however, some basic Premises which can be made.

These concern:
- ✓ Existence of an All-powerful GOD
- ✓ Existence of Prophets who seek to tell GOD's message and to correct Mankind's Errors.
- ✓ GOD's Wrath Happens and Mankind Suffers.
- ✓ Man's Evil Ways bring Retribution.
- ✓ Mankind has a Choice, Free-Will is allowed.
- ✓ There is a Good and Loving Way Ahead.
- ✓ Spirits, Souls, Ghosts, Angels, do exist.
- ✓ There is a Life after Death.
- ✓ There is a Heaven, a Hell and many other Planes of Existence.
- ✓ We are part of Nature, if we disturb the Balance, Nature will react to correct this.
- ✓ We return through many Lifetimes to learn the Lessons necessary. This is NOT a one-off. Reincarnation is an essential feature of our Existence.
- ✓ We exist amongst a Peer Group of some 40-50 Souls, the Roles change from Lifetime to Lifetime so that we can have the opportunity of learning ALL aspects of LOVE.
- ✓ We Create, through our Actions, our own Environment and our own Karma, our own future level of Experience, be that Happiness or Suffering.
- ✓ We are not alone in the Universe, there are many other more intelligent Species.
- ✓ We are all Energy, we all Inter-react.
- ✓ What you do as an Individual affects those around you. It is all CAUSE and EFFECT.
- ✓ You pre-chose this Lifetime's Experience before you were born. You chose your parents. You chose the lessons for your Soul to learn. If you do not choose wisely now, you will have wasted this Lifetime and a repetition will become necessary, not only for you but also for those of your Peer-Group who need to be involved. You become locked into a 'Cycle of Repetition'.
- ✓ Nothing happens by Coincidence.
- ✓ Thoughts are as powerful as Actions - Beware !

1.16 These Sentiments are but a few from the many KEYPOINTS, which are listed throughout the Text. I make no apology for any repetition, as the Keypoints are drawn from the Life Experience whenever this has occurred.

A SYNOPSIS of the Book of Truth and Knowledge

This One Book of some 178,000 words is the first of three that are eventually to be written.
An Autobiography, drawing upon first-hand experience of this Lifetime, the story unfolds from one of a Human, Earthly, Materialistic Lifestyle, with a succession of broken marriages, heartbreak and children, through to a radical change in Behaviour and Spirituality, caused by a series of Human Experiences which involve each of three Psychic Partners.

This One Book, whether you believe it to be Fact or Fiction, sets out for Mankind a platform of Beliefs as to:
- How the Race Originated
- How Mankind should relate to GOD and to NATURE
- What the True Purpose for our Lives is.
...........and yet it is so much more!

It is claimed that the Book is Divinely Inspired, that it is written and named at the behest of High Spirit who work ceaselessly for GOD. Words are brought from GOD, from JESUS, from MARY, from WHITE EAGLE, from a succession of Spirit Guides, also from PRINCESS DIANA, and ISAIAH.

This One Book challenges a number of the traditional Christian Beliefs, such as the Trinity and portrays Jesus as being a Man with a Child. The Author claims to have lived 77 Lives on the Earth, and to be the re-incarnation of John the Apostle who wrote the Gospel and the Revelations. Many other Lives are claimed to have all originated from the One Soul.
The Human Life is seen as a Training Ground for the recovery of Dark Souls back to Union with GOD. The Book warns the Race that unless there is a significant shift towards Love, Compassion, Humanity and Respect for Creation, that the Future will be filled with disaster.
Many aspects of Human Life are commented upon, Transplants for example, Smoking, the Cause for many diseases and illnesses, the power of Thought, the power of LOVE.
The Writer tells of the Birth of a New Messiah in the new Millennium.

A Section is presented to help the Reader along the Pathway to Communication with their own Soul and with GOD.
The Book is written in the format of a Teaching Reference, with KEYPOINTS of Learning and Understanding drawn from the Text and the Personal Experiences

This article has been used as a Press Release in 2002

INSPIRED MESSAGES

The following Messages are taken from the Book of Truth and Knowledge, and have been assembled as a Booklet for ALL to see. Messages are published from
- WHITE EAGLE, the Spirit Guide and Messenger
- JESUS, the Prophet and Christ
- MARY, the Mother of Jesus
- GOD, the Supreme Power
- PRINCESS DIANA, whose Life was tragically taken, now a Helper
- ISAIAH, the Biblical Prophet

The heading numbers refer to the Chapter in the Book of Truth and Knowledge from which they are taken.

Explanatory Notes

(a) Chapter break. ~~~~~~
(b) Keypoints in bold –
 These are learning points from the text.
(c) *{Italics}* Author (John) comments to clarify context.

messages from WHITE EAGLE.

[White Eagle acts as a Messenger on behalf of the Group of Five High Spirit who seek to prevent Mankind from destroying the World and the Race. White Eagle is an old Friend of mine from Past Lives, and from the present Work, which we do together in Spirit.]

6.49 I am asked in the middle of the Night, by White Eagle, the words come through Helana:
'What is more important, one man or the future of the Earth?...I respond that no one Individual is more important than the whole of Mankind.
I am also asked: 'where would I prefer to sit? at the head of the Table, or to the right of Jesus?'... I do not fully understand either question, but respond that to the right of the Lord Jesus is acceptable to me!

6.54 White Eagle asks, when I am half-asleep in Bed: 'if you could invite some people to a Dinner-Party, whom would you like to invite? I think back to my previous relationships, and do not wish to upset Helana or offend anyone else by leaving them out. I think for ten seconds, I respond that I would like to invite all those who love and have loved me! I then fell asleep. Little did I anticipate the problems and antagonism that my response would create.
In retrospect, perhaps I should have taken ten hours to decide upon my reply!
The Banquet took place, without my mind being aware of this. I am told that at a future Time, when my full Awareness has been achieved, that I will be able to recall this occasion.
Some two hundred Individuals were present, stretching back through Time over my seventy-seven Human Lives. Chaos, Jealousy, Hate, Spite, Unpleasantness were all present; for many there who had not met with their adversaries or protagonists, since their original involvement with me took place. Wives, ex-wives, Lovers, Mistresses... Helana was put-out, Spirit were not too pleased.

I was surprised when told that the order of Seating at the Table reflected their individual depth of Love for me... see Appendix VII. in the BOOK OF TRUTH AND KNOWLEDGE, for the initial Seating Plan.

6.55 The following Day, Helana brings to me the following words from White Eagle:
'John, we wish to say all is as it should be my dear Man, and your Thoughts have been noted on many occasions. We brought to you last Night-time a lesson in the power of thought, what is needed now is for you to apply your mind as to how this meeting will have affected those who were present at your Table. The Lord Jesus had prepared one similar in past Times to share with his Disciples all that he could offer in the way of re-assurance to these men of Life-everlasting, and to emphasize his continued presence in their Lives even beyond all that could be seen by their own Eyes at that Time.
We had hoped my dear Man, that your speech to those around your Table would have contained a gift for the future years, which would have helped these Spirits find reassurance within their own Hearts for their future Pathways...

We feel for the time your Lady is absent from your Day, in the future Days to come, you should reflect on how your Thoughts and Actions can and Do affect the Lives of Others, and how much in this Life has changed from that of Past-Lives, to change what has become part of your True Nature.'

KEYPOINTS TP34
a) Thoughts on the Earth-Plane help to create our Future World and Experiences.
b) Thoughts in the Spirit World act to create the Present.
c) Thoughts are as powerful as Actions, accordingly they need to be controlled.

~~~~~~

7.21 Read frequently, the words displayed in your Hall, given by White Eagle:
'If you live Tranquilly and Patiently, always with the Consciousness of GOD's love upholding you, you will find that all your Life will be Heaven. Whatever has crept into, and seemingly spoilt your Life will all gradually be resolved. But this won't happen if you harbour Irritation, Fear and Chaos in your own Heart.
Let go these futile worries and fears my Children.
All things work together for good for him (or her), who loves GOD.'

~~~~~~

8.44 A message is then given to Helana from White Eagle: 'Look at the World as a Whole; a small Happening, which is happening to you, can change the World. You can heal Ireland alone with your Love. You will need to visit each Area, to heal that Area and that Community. Both John and you have a vital role to play. I apologize for past misrepresentation.
To explain fully about the Child would take a long Time. It may be that a Child is not necessary; each action of each Person dictates these things. Continue with your Faith. We wish to prepare you for the coming of a Child, in case that Child is necessary. We cannot say whether a Child will be needed or not.
World Events are such that we need to be ready. It is complicated my Dear. We only ask that you live your Life, and if we feel the need is there, then it will be you to whom the Child is sent. We talk also to you John in this respect. Do not allow it to mar your relationship. Do not feel used. I cannot fully understand the Human Emotions involved, it is many years since I came to Earth as a living Being. Rest assured my Dear, no outside Spirit will be tampering with you. If you feel this is so, look again, and understand yourself more deeply.......we will be with you and will be watching. The Spirits that have troubled and invaded you and been a nuisance to your Body will not trouble you again'.

KEYPOINTS D34
a) **Healing of Spirit and Body, can take place merely through the presence of God's Healing Power, as at this Time the Holy Spirit was present within Helana, it was simply necessary for her to pass through an Area, in order for Healing to occur.**
b) **By allowing People to feel the presence of Love, their attitudes can be changed, and so the possibility of change and reconciliation between Peoples can occur.**

8.45 'We ask of John a little more study, a little more calmness and a little more discipline in his Mind, and in his Lifestyle. Not to change his Lifestyle, but more of these Things will enable him to See, and to Hear, far more quickly. We look forward to the time when he can bring these messages. We ask that he does his utmost to stop Earthly Things taking so much precedence; we realize these are important, they can be achieved, but also, at a moment's notice he can be with Spirit. It is of great importance that he hears every word and brushes nothing aside. In this Lifetime, each meeting, each person, each event will be of importance. In order to hear and see, do try and calm your Mind. It is easier to help Others in a Spiritual manner, if they see a calmness in you. Allow Others to see this, you may then bustle-off!'

KEYPOINTS D35
a) **A calmness in your Mind is an essential feature of good communication with Spirit.**
b) **Spirit can and do arrange all key meetings and events; they can even control the speed of a vehicle to ensure a key meeting or event takes place, nothing happens by pure chance or coincidence.**
c) **A balance is necessary at all times between Earthly and Spiritual Work.** *{Spirit wish me to commit more fully to their Work and the Learning necessary for my Spiritual Awareness to develop. This is difficult when I still need to feed and house myself, pay maintenance, and service my Debts!}*

8.46 'We thank Judith for her hard Work. Look and see the time that was necessary to bring forward Helana. We ask you Three to do this for Others. Earthly Things are of minor Importance once you have taken the Steps necessary. We wait to welcome you fully to the Spiritual Life. It is also the Time now, to tell you that we are withdrawing Judith for a period of Time. She is not aware of this, but there is work to be done elsewhere. Be of an understanding if she cancels an appointment, or is unable to see you. She looks forward to coming to Ireland and working with you, John. This may be the case, but if she is successful with the work elsewhere, she will not be with you in Ireland'.

8.47 'You may now rejoice, as we do here in Spirit, for the Love found between you both. You will be as One from now to Eternity. No man will be able to put aside this Coupling. We wish you both Love, Peace, Understanding and Clarity of Mind at all Times. Thank you for your Time, and follow the Words given'.

8.48 'Helana's presence is needed in Ireland. The need is now. Make plans to be in Ireland as quickly as possible. We ask that you work hard to be in Ireland. Time is limited. I reiterate the previous words…This is a major necessity to World Events. A place of residence will be shown. We ask this of you John. A greater Understanding will be given of anything which is not clear at the Outset. If you live frugally, your expenses can be met. We ask: 'What is better? The World and all that you know, or, a full meal on your plate within your own Home? This comes as a dramatic request to your Minds… the need is thus. We would drop pennies from Heaven, if we could to help you. Go forwards with haste. A great happening is to come about.'
KEYPOINTS D36
a)`Timing is of the Essence. To be in the right Place, at the correct Time, is sometimes necessary when Events of Worldly magnitude are likely to happen.`
{High Spirit have told us that they do not trust in the decisions which the American President, Bill Clinton might take. The wrong decision could lead to an explosion in World Events, which could precipitate a reaction from Russia, China, Iran, Iraq, Korea, or even Nature itself. High Spirit wish us to be in Ireland not only for the Spirit Healing, but also for our own Safety.}

8.49 White Eagle continues: 'You have a slight Vision of a New World emerging. That World……the Time allocated for that World to come into being, runs short. You merrily strolled the roads and lanes in Ireland, little comprehending the major necessity for your presence. We do not wish to strike fear in your Hearts, but, the cogs which turn are wearing-out. The work is to be done from this moment. Spend time Helana with your visions, and your Heart focussed solely on Ireland and Eire as a whole. We thank you for this evening, recognizing that how can a Heart Center be sliced down the middle. It would not beat.! We realize that you need also to live your Earthly life'.

8.50 'We ask that you, Helana, set aside at least one hour per evening to concentrate your Mind, your Body and your whole Being on the Heart-Center of the Earth.(Ireland) ….that you walk and continue to walk in Ireland, until your days on Earth are over. There is much afoot beyond your comprehension. The state of Ireland is dire, and this is indicative of the situation on the Earth-Plane'.

KEYPOINT D37
Ireland is at the Heart of the World. If the Heart is healed, then the Body has a chance to be healed. The Heart will not be healed fully whilst it is divided. Ultimately, the two halves will need to unite.

8.51 'We ask of John too, that he will allow you to concentrate on this Work. He too is needed in Ireland. We are pleased ,although we jest and joke and send strange messages.....
We are very delighted by the progress he has made. Do not lose your strength of character, John, but we ask that you seek the calmness within, and show to the outside World a jovial, and likeable character. Judith has given to us that you do slowdown your pace of Life and Mind. We require of you a Jeckel and Hyde existence. Do not speak of these matters until a signal is given. We need calmness, for our benefit, to allow us to hear you.
You do not appreciate the difficulty we have, the draining of our Energy it takes to come to the Earth-Plane. Your Planet is so low in energy vibration, it is so difficult to come here, I puff, I pant, it is so Dark here...but, I come because I work for the true-Being, I work for the Holy-Light, but of a brilliance so great you may be blinded.'

KEYPOINT D38
It can help High Spirit to remain close, more easily, on the Earth-Plane, when a Candle is lit. Remember though, that Candle-Light will attract ALL Spirit.

8.52 'If I sound pompous, forgive me for I do not wish to.....only to explain the differences. Imagine if you will, I walk normally in the most brilliant of sunshine; I come only in matters of great Importance to the type of Light you may find at Dusk. You are both the loveliest of People who come together in unison.
Things have been said of you, which must have been hurtful, however, you still continue to move forwards, and when your eyes are truly open, we look forward to welcoming you. The importance of this mission is beyond your comprehension. Do not fear that you will both be protected and cared for'.

8.53 'I am not able, here in Spirit, to completely comprehend the human emotions and needs related to you as a Couple, blessed by Spirit with a Love so profound. There need never be any doubt between you as to where the other's Earthly Heart is placed and will remain. I have returned with a message, in the hope that John will understand most fully'.
'When two Earth people come together in the way that has been blessed by the highest of Spirit, then there can be no Time apart from each other, but that is not in a Bodily fashion. Your Spirits are entwined forever, so have no doubt that if Helana is not within Earthly vision or presence, it simply means her Body is not there.

It is the case that each of you is being asked to work for Spirit. At any given Time, each of you could be doing entirely different Earthly or Spiritual work; but trust John; that your whole Spiritual Beings are together. If one is doing an Earthly job and the other does not approve, it matters not.! Neither of you should question what the Other does. It is to be the case that we require Helana to sit and think of Ireland.....Do not be put-out John, understand that as two vibrations working on a single Task, they may become blurred. Compare this to a Radio Frequency, an overlap of Stations can occur. It is the same with two Spirits, they will not concentrate in the same manner. We ask you John to sit alone... un-interrupted. We ask you to do Spirit work at that Time... do not allow any feelings of Hurt to enter any part of your Being, that is not the case.

The great work will enable the Spirit of Helana to rise and to reside in the Future with you John'.

KEYPOINTS D39

a) There exists around our Being an Energy field (Aura) which reacts to and is changed by other Energy fields, People or Machines or Nature. Whenever you pass close to or beneath Electricity Pylons for example, you need to ask for a protective Shield to surround you.

b) Your own Aura and Spirit may be affected by, or may become dependant upon, another close to you. It may be necessary, when each of you needs to contact their own Guides, or to work Independently, for you to physically separate for this work to continue.

c) Your Spirits may be together, even though your Bodies are not.

d) Each individual has an Aura, the collective combination of all Humans produce an Aura which emanates from the Earth-Plane and affects Other Planets throughout the Universe. The Aura which emanates from the Earth is Dark and Negative and indicative of a dominance of Evil. This is why the present Work and the need for Change is so pressing. If you have a bad Apple in the Barrel, what do you do?.....The Earth-Plane is viewed by Alien Species as the Bad Apple. Fortunately, we now have time to heal the Core, and grow a new Healthy Apple! If we do not succeed, then the Earth-Plane will not exist as such; we can then expect another Atlantis or Noah Situation to develop.

KEYPOINTS D40
a) Do not under-Estimate the effect that YOUR contribution can make. Consider the Nuclear Explosion, whenever a critical mass is established, the whole will rapidly change.
b) The ONE (You) can make all the difference.
c) HEAVEN ON EARTH will be established when the critical mass of LOVE and COMPASSION is established on the Earth-Plane

~~~~~~

10.57 It is Saturday, 29th August 1998. Judith and Helana sit huddled-up against the 'cold' created by the presence of so many Spirits. I am told that members of our Families for the past 2,000 years are present, by invitation of High Spirit, to witness the proceedings. They are brought this day together for them to understand what it is that we are doing, to give to them knowledge of our trust, our commitment and our belief. By seeing this, each One of them will rise higher in the Sphere of Spirit, having glimpsed the Glory that can be. White Eagle is to speak through Judith, to his right hand Side stands Bob, behind them stand four High Spirit, two each side. Jesus kneels before Judith.
'My Dears, I hope that I may come fully with my Voice, I have now come forward to bring such a Message, even I do not have it, it has been two blinks of the Eye since I last spoke with my own Voice... This... that is better, the Child relaxes more that I may come more easily for you... Welcome, welcome, I look upon this... I am not happy with my voice... Forgive me... (.pause)... We will proceed regardless.
(Judith stroking her Throat)
I welcome you, I thank you and wish you to relate all to your Friend upon her return. (*Judith's Spirit has left her Body and has been replaced by the Spirit of White Eagle*)
My Dears, your trust and your faith and commitment and your beliefs have been sorely tested... We welcome those from Spirit to join us to witness what is to be... The coming together of your friend's Spirit with that of the Man. Bear in mind the importance of this. These Spirits were first parted at the beginning of all of You. *(Adam and Eve as in Genesis)*

Do not however be fearful for each Human Body will walk their chosen path on the Earth-Plane, until such time they are recalled to the World we call Spirit. These two Spirits are to be joined as One, never to be parted. Together in every Life... should they choose to return... they will find each Other and know the Other instantly.
The Human side is a little more difficult for them, only because they are Human, and each Human having their own very strong... it is the way of them... their personality, they have strong personalities, but each also has such deep Love for Mankind... this Lady smokes.......gestures!!!

17

They will come together as a beautiful couple, but at times it will be tense...we will smooth the way. Try my Dears...we are helping each of you as best we can......for their Spirits stand here behind Jesus....to be joined with such beauty, such Love, such strength and such power. Your Friends can see (*hand gestures*) the gold Ribbon which signifies these Spirits remain together for Eternity.....is bound around them by the Lord Jesus who comes as a symbol for the People gathered who are able to understand Jesus...For you, the things you are to achieve, relate so strongly to this Man who walked your Earth and died to be remembered, to never be forgotten. How sad he suffered for us. Now, to have to do this again.

KEYPOINTS BTB37
a) Spirits can divide and can be re-United.
b) The Strength and Power of the combined Spirit is greater than the separate Parts.

10.58 'The way ahead will not always be easy. Earthly emotions mar certain functions within you. We do all we can to help you to appreciate this, that your Earthly emotions may be understood by each one of you, that you come to a clear understanding of yourselves. In this way all becomes Lighter, the burdens become Lighter, the World becomes Lighter. We now move-on.'

KEYPOINT BTB38
a) Your individual actions can affect everyone else.
b) As you gain Spiritual Awareness and Understanding of yourself and your emotions; So your Spirit becomes Lighter, So your burdens and baggage become less, So the Aura of the Earth is lightened.

10.59 'My Dears I am an old Man,.....this girl's Body does not fit me......I like laughter....I struggle, I so wanted this to be completely my Voice....to know that I would not come lightly to this Room. You are correct...there is a Shadow which hovers over this Town.
(*Banbury has a darkness created by its History, starting with the Druids and continued by the Plague and Civil War etc.*)
We have first to say goodbye to the visitors...we thank them for coming and hope they have enjoyed their visit, and have seen the joining of the perfect Spirit... forgive me Bob. I cannot lie "Together you can move Mountains." ....

10.60 'Welcome Helana and John, I wish you were able to see we have another Visitor brought here for the two of You. I introduce the Angel Gabriel, who is to pass his Blessing on each of You. We, I am preparing to recede slightly that your Friend may see the Visitor and tell You later...but please in this instant try, try to see yourself. He has come to bring you the most precious Gift known. Let no Man, or no Spirit tell you differently.

Walk together along your chosen Path, but my Dears we have chosen it for you. Do not let that detract from the Courage and Strength you have shown in letting us guide you. The gift of the Child is within. The Angel Gabriel encompasses the Babe that it may grow into the beautiful Child you have been shown. Who else put this loving Man as the Father?
I known to Others as White Eagle, join you also in a Love so strong that there may never be any doubts or concerns.......You are of the Earth.

There will be those Moments...Do not let them fester so the wound is not too great to Heal. All can be healed by Love to enable you to 'make good' again' ...{I thank White Eagle.....He smiles and claps his Hands}
'It is as old Friends being re-united'

10.61 'Your Friend Judith is so joyous at meeting with Bob again after so long...I Thought...I may not overcome that strong Spirit. This brings us to a most important part of these Proceedings.....the Strength of the Spirit, whilst joined with the other half is all powerful. Therefore it follows that this...for instance, will only be possible should the joined Spirit fully allow Another to enter the Body.
At normal times, a Spirit, particularly a higher Spirit can quite easily, not remove the Spirit of a human Body, but lift it, allowing the Higher Spirit to enter. A darkened Spirit cannot simply enter, it can only enter if invited and allowed to be there; whereas a higher Spirit can uplift the host Spirit and enter in to give a Message...but even this is difficult if both the Mind and Spirit of the host Body do not wish this...but it can still be done. Helana had a problem only because she allowed that to happen...I only mention this as a comparison.'
KEYPOINTS BTB39
a) Dark Spirit cannot 'take-over' your Being unless you are a willing Host.
b) Higher Spirit can, if they so choose, enter your Being by 'lifting' your Spirit for a short period of time.

10.62 'Again, we have to request that you continue to behave with your Friend, Judith, in a normal manner.....for, the way she is on the Earth-Plane is most beautiful, maybe not to all men, but we see within her, she is pure Spirit, but for all that she still needs the Earthly Love of you both...as this has been a considerable amount for her Earthly Mind to contend with. *(The Angel leaves having blessed each One and the Child)* I thank you for allowing this to happen, as I leave be ready to assist your Friend.'

10.63 'I return my Dears.....Helana, John, have your Spirits not previously been joined? .....wrapped around with the Golden Band. Did this Ceremony not take place for You?
This Joining on this Occasion....which I give my humble apologies for not making it more clear, was the Joining of Judith with her half-Spirit Bob......... 'Now the Spirits are as One'
White Eagle continues: 'You may wonder as to why I did not refer to the Man by the name you know him on Earth...He in a previous life was my wife!... I therefore find it most difficult to refer to him by the name now chosen.....You understand that his Spirit was the lady I took for my wife.

I apologise, but however hard I try, I cannot think of that Spirit as a man...that Spirit is so beautiful...I am sentimental, but take it that it is Bob. Do not forget that you John, and Helana, are joined as these two are joined.'

10.67 White Eagle states that 'Helana is beautiful not only in Spirit but also in her Being.........She is:
- As the Deer in the Forest
- As the Breeze in the Trees
- As the Warmth of the Sun
- As a Light in the Stars
- As the Glow of the Moon

10.68 Jupiter is the Planet of Law and Order for the Universe.'

~~~~~~

11.22 White Eagle later comes through, we have checked into a Guest House near the Town Centre, 'All is as it should be. You have been guided and have followed well. The house chosen by you to rent in Ballyholme (*a District within Bangor*) is the one intended. It is basic, but Helana can transform this. The choice of position will assist the clarity of your communication with us. This is only intended as a temporary home, for better things are to come. We are sorry that it was necessary to interfere with your TV reception in order to bring this message. We needed to bring this now in order to re-assure Helana. Helana has done well, her Prayers have lifted the Areas we have driven through and many Souls have been recovered.
KEYPOINT IR12
Spirit can and do affect your environment. TV reception, Telephone bells, flickering electric lights, elongated candle-flames, to name just a few.{Our TV screen in the Hotel was wiped-out in the middle of a Film, to cause me to accept a Message from Spirit.

On other occasions, my Telephone would not stop ringing,(to prevent its use) and my car radio tape-deck became silent(to restart later}

11.25 Helana receives the following from White Eagle 'Helana my Dear, your efforts are an example my Dear of how great your dedication is to this Man and the work for Spirit. Now we ask you to feel the comfort of your Homeland as now you have entered the coming of the Promised Land. You have had a fractious Journey with many hazards you have not been aware of. We say now that you will receive peace of Mind knowing that the rest of your Stay will not be so fraught.'

11.26 'Your Man is suffering at this present time, but Understanding is being given and we are pleased to see his acceptance of this. Your Journey is not complete but understand yours is as one with that of Mary, and her husband to be. Understand there are many similarities and we wish you to record these! Your husband's pains (John) will disappear on understanding that we wish him to take more charge of his own Life as regards to his Spiritual Understanding, and learning to help himself. We realize this is not easy but help will be given.
Go now my Dear with new Understanding in your Spirit and allow us to guide you safely on your way. Remember my Dear that you are protected at all times and your husband also. He is suffering, but all is for Lessons to be learnt by himself, and these will be invaluable in the future years with his work to be for Spirit.
Let our Hearts rejoice in your presence in this Land, for already your work has begun and the cloud has been lifted....Go in Peace my Dears and rejoice in the Child who resides within your Womb, awaiting the birth of this glorious Age; one to be treasured and remembered for all Mankind.'

11.31 White Eagle writes: 'My Dear, your man's Spirit is now with you in the fullest way; no more will you be sharing this man with memories of the Past or present Life situations. He has no Understanding of the way in which his Spirit feels. We ask you now to pass on this message in its entirety for him to gain an Understanding. Your Love my Dear has been constant throughout Time and History, never failing this man in any capacity. Believe these words John, to gain an Understanding of the depth of Love this Lady has for you; not on any occasion will it fail you in any way. A dedication such as this will be felt throughout the Universe my dear Man; Look and see beyond the face, beyond the skin my dear Man. Do you not see the true beauty of your Woman who is and will be forever your Love, forever your Lady, and always has been. No other can, has, or will be.!' Go now with this knowledge in your Heart and do not ever give-up understanding fully this message.
KEYPOINT IR16
Your Thoughts and Actions on the Earth-Plane can have an Effect throughout the Universe.

11.32 'My Dear, your strength amazes us still. Will you now my Dear understand why your presence is so important in this Land. We are expecting so much from your Spirit. We push and push not realizing how much pain you can bear my Dear, but still you seem to take on all that is given. Not only do you take on your own pains of the Past, but those of your Man and this Land. Also, Understanding is not always present within your Mind, but in time this will be found more quickly. You have now the Feelings of all that has been within your Past Lives with this Man, and we feel that you are now of an Understanding that sadness has played a major role in all of them. You can now go forwards my Dear with the Knowledge that all present within your Lives in future years will be happiness and Love.'

11.33 'Do not doubt your abilities in coping with what is brought to your Man. You are coping admirably. You have full protection my Dear in all matters and we feel now your greatness in this ability to overcome Obstacles will stand you in good stead for the Future........Your Man's pains are those feelings of the Past which you have shared, for he still has more discovering to do about the past Lives shared, for the Understanding is not yet complete.'

KEYPOINT IR17
The Spirit never forgets, and pain from previous Lifetimes can be returned for Healing and Understanding.

11.34 'You have been given all of these Spirits from your previous Relationships my Dear as a final clearing of the ways, to begin again, a new Life, a new Spirit and a new togetherness that will be with you throughout Eternity and beyond all your comprehension. Do not feel endangered in any way, it was necessary to clear the ways before this new Life would begin, and for the closeness shared to be seen in the fullest way. We now will see a marked improvement in the way your Togetherness will come about and the sharing of your lives, and every movement will be a treasure to behold. Go now my Dear with peace in your Heart, knowing that all is clear for your pathway to be free from all obstacles. Let us now guide you through your years'...White Eagle

KEYPOINTS IR18
a) Re-birth of your Spirit is a wondrous event, when the Past is wiped clean, so that there are no restrictions on the growth of your Spirit.
b) Following re-birth, you can expect to see Spirit, to hear Spirit Audibly, to see visions in the near Future.

11.35 'Your Love has now been found and you are joined together in Love in this Land. You could have, and should have, achieved this in previous Lives. You originally realized your Love when you were Brother and Sister in a previous Life. Now you can Heal the Land and the Spirits around you...If you had come together in this way years ago, you could have done it then!'

KEYPOINT IR19
a) Love is the greatest Power.
b) If you do not achieve in one Lifetime, it will be returned in another; but many from your Peer Group will have to mark time until the desired result is achieved.

11.41 A few Days previously, White Eagle had come with these Words, whilst we admired the view in Killykeagh, Northern Ireland.
'Once upon a time there was a beautiful Princess. She became the treasure of the Land, her gift to the People was Love and in return her gift will be a home given with Love. All is returned, however many Lifetimes it takes, for <u>all</u> is remembered and nothing is lost, but <u>all</u> is gained. Look around you my Dears, this location could be Heaven on Earth if you so wish.'

~~~~~~

12.13 White Eagle writes.... 'The effect of the past Days is taking its toll, and you need to recuperate and renew your concentration. You can ask for Energy to be given, this will be; your Spirit will still need however to rest to recover to it's full strength. You have had a difficult time in Ireland and in transit to and from that Country. You have also had the problem of the message from Judith and the strain of the little Ones. We suggest that you rest tonight and we will take you in your sleep to bathe and rest. Do not be distressed all is as it should be. You have done well and are making good progress. World Events unfortunately, set their own agenda and we are obliged to react as quickly as we can. Forgive us my Dears if we press you so much, you appreciate now the importance of your work and every support will be given to assist you, and to relieve the stress. Imagine yourself surrounded by a white Light and that Light pulsating slowly like a Lighthouse. Feel the energy enter as the Light pulsates.
Clear your Mind of Daily worries and troubles, and sit quietly to relieve your tensions. This will help you both to find relaxation. Go to your Bed now, and we will talk later when you feel more refreshed.'

KEYPOINTS TD11
a) You can Pray and ask for Energy.
b) You can condition your Body and your Mind by using your thoughts to help you to relax, and to relieve your stress.

c) Your Spirit becomes tired, and can need rest to recuperate, in the same way that your bodily Being does.
d) Imagine yourself surrounded by a sphere of white Light which pulsates slowly. As the Light pulsates, visualize the energy flowing into you.

12.14 White Eagle writes to Helana: My Dear, the People of Ireland cry out for your Love and the Peace that prevails whilst your presence is felt. You have indeed no Understanding at this Time what this Awareness achieves. We do understand my Dear how much we ask of you at this time, but we feel your urgency to be within the Land of your chosen Pathways.
All now will proceed and you will be within this Land in time for your Christmas Celebration. All we ask of You at this Time my dear Helana, is that your Thoughts reach out to the Peoples of this Land; bring to them the Understanding that your Presence has not been withdrawn, only halted for a short time. We hope this helps with your Understanding, and we ask your Man to contact his own Guides, for guidance as to what is to be achieved. All your Lives my Dear, have been a preparation for this farewell-end to a glorious Life, shared with all the Peoples of this World. Go in peace my Dear.'

12.15 'Helana my Dear, understand what is in hand, is very urgent to secure the Lives of many people. Your apprehension is due to the knowledge of the work involved for your loved one. This knowledge is within but not known to his Mind. Do not fear this time my Dear, for your protection is guaranteed at all times, you are aware of this.
The children my Dear, Edwin and Helen will perhaps have other plans which will enable you to see clearly what is needed. We ask a great deal of you all at this time, but understand the Earth and its needs will not wait. Your Guides are by your side my Dear, and communications will become clearer very shortly. Forget now my Dear your Personal Problems for the time being, to see what is needed for the beloved Community of our Earth-Plane. Go with Peace my Dear'.

12.22 White Eagle writes..... 'picture Helana as a flower in bud in the Desert, trying to grow without moisture, imagine the pain and suffering. You John, have the nourishment of her Love, she needs the nourishment of your Love before she can become a wonderful flower. The flower (Helana) is then able to nourish the World'. Your left-Shoulder pain is given to remind you that the final piece of the puzzle is not yet fitted (ie my love for Helana), a small pain alongside that of the World. Helana has sacrificed and suffered much for you, she has been prepared to push you to your awareness. Think of your leg-pains following the Company Charity wheel-chair push. If you John had walked away as Philip does, then you too could have ended up in a wheel-Chair like the man Trevor!'

KEYPOINTS TD17
a) **Our Human choices can well affect the State of our Health!** *(the man Trevor is confined to a Wheel Chair following an Accident, which was given as a direct result of his repeated Philandering and the devastation caused to Others Lives)*
b) **Spirit are aware of all our pain and suffering.**

12.23 'We now see the 'perfect Being' arising out of Helana, for this reason we presented her with the Holy Spirit. Do not fear this. Do not worry that you cannot live-up to her expectations, she accepts fully that You are as You are. With Faith and Trust, you John will not be made to feel above or below her. No harm will come to your Spirit. Open-up your eyes and see there is no judgement in Helana's eyes, only dedication and honesty. Trust her, look beneath the surface. You are her Life, her one and only, she has no fear of this. Only sadness is felt perhaps for those left behind.'

KEYPOINTS TD18
a) **The Gift of the Holy Spirit is quite exceptional, and should not be confused with our normal Spiritual Awareness, or Knowledge from our Spirit Guides.**
b) **The Gift of the Holy Spirit imparts special Powers and a special relationship with GOD.....HELANA IS THE ONLY PERSON IN THE WORLD, TODAY, WITH THE HOLY SPIRIT.**

12.73 I make no apology for quoting this Message in full, from Helana's Guide, at this time White Eagle. (12.73 - 12.82)
'My Dear, your Bravery exceeds our Understanding. We do not expect miracles from Beings on this Earth-Plane my Dear, but your strength of Character far exceeds what we have believed possible for one so young to Spiritual Matters. This man John has no idea as yet what a Treasure he has been given. It was hoped your presence in his Life would bring to him Understanding of Spiritual Matters to help him progress. We have seen your dedication to this Cause and have therefore progressed his awareness accordingly. It was always intended to take place, that which has been given, but our hopes and expectations were for a new Life in the next Lifetime, having learned many lessons in this.'
{This was a Choice I was given on several Occasions, not to proceed in this Lifetime}

12.74 'The World's progress would have been halted somewhat, but plans were afoot to help this time, to support the Lives of the People, until such time as you would have returned.
It is clear to us now that this can be achieved in this Lifetime. We apologize if you see this as a lack of faith in your direction, but miracles have truly taken place and your determination my Dear sets a standard for All to follow.'

12.75 'Do not fear this, for it is possible for all Beings to climb the Ladder of Life if they wish, as you have shown to us here in Spirit. We do not expect this of Many, but nevertheless it can be achieved. There is great hope in the hearts of all Beings in this Universe for what they see as real and promising, to allow the Peoples of the Earth-Plane time enough to discover what is needed.'
KEYPOINT TD44
a) All Spirit have the opportunity to progress their Understanding and the level of their Awareness.
b) The passage tells of the existence of other Beings within the Universe, and implies that the actions of Mankind are being monitored by some of these other 'Alien' peoples.

12.76 'Your Children within learn rapidly my Dear, and will continue their mother's work into future generations. Nothing is lost my Dear and although your feelings are somewhat distant, do not doubt your worth, for your Love is present and sent out to many Peoples at this time.
Your sickness is almost over my Dear, this has provided you with the time needed for your rest so deserved. You are not aware of how much you achieve throughout your Day my Dear, constantly using your Spirit to project truth and honesty to all who will hear. Do not compare with Others my Dear, for they too have their own ways in which they work. Understand, a Life of Giving has been for your Spirit, it is now time for those around you to give back something in return. Do not expect miracles my Dear but understand and recognize what is being given'.
KEYPOINT TD45
Our Lives are pre-Planned, and all that happens to us is Known and Controlled...even to the extent of a Cold!

12.77 'The Time now lends itself, to providing you my Dear, a peaceful occasion where you may gather in all that has been lost along the way. Your Spirit sees a great deal and more is to be forthcoming. Lessons for John have been harsh, but it has proved necessary to bring to him these Lessons in such a way, for his armour-plating around his Heart is thick and strong.
We have found the only way to break through this barrier is to Shock, and to show to him in vision what his actions cause, and what neglectful ways will create.

Your suffering has caused him pain and anguish, but at last we feel we have broken through, and a fear of losing what is so precious to him, has now prompted his Spirit to rise from the depths of Isolation. Understanding, that not to do so would cause such anguish and pain to Others. One so beautiful in our Eyes, would be such a loss to this World, and he has now realized the true wealth of your Spirit in his eyes.'

KEYPOINT TD46
The harshness of our suffering can be adjusted, if this is necessary, in order to teach us the lessons our Spirits need to learn! The more stubborn you are, the more resistant to change, the harsher will become the lessons.

12.78 'All is now complete my Dear, You will begin to feel alive again, for my Dear you have been slowly dying within, encompassed by such loneliness and such feelings, yet again so alone. Your Spirit cannot survive my Dear in this way, you are in need of constant Love to enable you to feel alive. Your Man must understand this and realize that if he cannot bring to you these feelings, then Others must enable you to survive. It does not mean he is in danger of losing you, quite the contrary, he will gain a great deal from sharing with so many; for as you are aware your Love will be raised, and will be able to enlighten your man's Spirit, to the extent that his true Feelings will be revealed'.

12.79 'He has not yet experienced the Love of Spirit within his Spirit my Dear, but it is only now a few short moments away, and when this has been realized there will be no turning back. As you are aware, no Love is felt as strongly as Spiritual Love....these words may be passed on to your man my Dear, for he will recognize the signs as the words are read. His Spirit is awakened my Dear and his feelings for you deepen each Day. It is hoped that a Night apart, will bring to your man's Mind the true closeness felt by your presence, that has not been found with another Being that has shared his Lifetimes.'

12.80 'We here in Spirit, John, sometimes have to make Life so hard for you, for your stubbornness of the Mind needs to be broken down. Understanding that cannot be found in a gentler way; needs to be introduced in these hard ways. Understand that these Lessons are given with Love, for you to find-out what we know is necessary for your Spirit. Stubbornness of Mind creates your Suffering, and Suffering to those closest to you, but in the end Lessons are learned, and your True Spirit is found. It is hoped a greater Understanding will have then been found for your progress with the Work that lies ahead. '

12.81 'All is a preparation my dear Man, but it is your choices and the pathways that you choose that can cause delay and suffering. But at the same time, all is needed for you to gain the Understanding and Knowledge needed for your ultimate role in the Lifetime allocated to your Spirit. You will be given a choice upon your return to Spirit, to either stay with your Lady in a different form, or to return to this Earth-Plane...To visit again, and to retain your closeness, and also to help Others find the same. Your other choices will be either to return to your Host-Planets, or to become Angels.'

KEYPOINTS TD47
a) We do choose our Lives, and the purpose for our Lives, before we are born.
b) Some Spirits choose to return to the Earth-Plane in order to help Others.
c) Some Spirits originally came to the Earth-Plane from other Planets....The Human Race is formed from 'Alien' Spirits.
d) Some Spirits can choose to become Angels.

12.82 'Whichever Pathway you both choose to follow, Understand you will always retain the Bond of being entwined as one Spirit, and not in any future Lifetime will your Journey be as long and as hard as it has been to find this beautiful Bonding that has now been achieved.
We hope now you will not become complacent and will continue to seek; Understanding fully all the implications that have been given, for nothing is secure unless diligence of Mind and Spirit are fully aware of how fragile Life can be on this Earth-Plane. One slip of the tongue can take your Spirit back many paces, only to have to recover them again. You will by now, feeling as you do, feel a little relieved that your loved-One is safe from ending the Life of this Lifetime. Always remember the fragility of this Spirit if Love is withdrawn, but remember also the strength of her commitment to you and your Life, even at the risk of her own. Go in Peace now, and retain these words in your Mind for your Spirit to fully Understand what has been gained that could so easily be lost.' {this ends the Message written by Helana and received from White Eagle}.

12.83 I am feeling the Spirit presence of Lorna and Constance around my Head; they come to learn about my Feelings, they know that they have lost my Love and the Chains of the Past are broken. They come for Understanding and Compassion. I am asked to say prayers for these Ladies. Present also are the Spirits of Mervin, Abel, Steven, Helana's mother, Mary, Ford, Alan, Albert and Cleanort. I ask who is Cleanort?

KEYPOINTS TD48
a) **Prayers can provide comfort and healing, and demonstrate compassion for Others.**
b) **Spirit come to you to learn about your feelings, for understanding, to give and to receive Love, and for compassion.**

12.84 'Cleanort was your child when you were married to Helana and lived at a town called Tanthea in Greece. Your name was Andrecius and you were Governor of this Region. (206-144bc.), Helana was known as Percarnia and your other Children were Marcia (Ford) and Adrenia (Brian). Cleanort was lost in Miscarriage and has remained in Spirit ever since.
The Child has never known a Human life; the Trauma of the first miscarriage was too much for this Spirit to handle without extreme distress. He has now accepted the situation of a Spirit-life and is content. He can take any age or form, and you choose to see him as an 8 year old Child.'

KEYPOINTS TD49
a) **Spirits are present within unborn children, and up to six weeks prior to conception the Spirit is within the Mother.**
b) **The Spirit is affected by trauma and experience whilst within the mother, all emotions and feelings are detected.**
c) **Not all Spirit choose to come to Earth for their Growth; not all Spirit choose to grow.**

12.115 It is October 2nd. 1998...We are formally requested by Spirit to change our Names from Dennis to JOHN, and from Alison to HELANA... For simplicity in this Book, I have chosen to use these Names throughout. 'Great works are to be achieved my Dear from this Day onwards...White Eagle is with you'.

12.116 'All praise should be given at this time my dear Helana, for your great Achievement in moving your Spirit from Darkness into Light in so few years...the Stars are yours my Dear, believe all that is written, for at no time will knowledge enter your Mind from Others around you... many of whom are so jealous and have interfered with many of your previous Life-times'.

12.117 'When you pray use the address. 'Dear Heavenly Father'...
All Prayers are heard and acted upon. Take care with your Requests, and ask only for Guidance and Assistance from the one Source known to you as GOD.'
{I have asked the question as to who prays should be addressed to, to GOD, to Jesus, to a Prophet. White Eagle responds as here stated}

13.23 White Eagle delivers this Message... 'You John, need to find the trust in High Spirit which Helana shows...She is largely self-taught by learning to understand the nature of Others. She places herself in danger, knowing that we are with her, guiding her. Let the beauty of Life fill your eyes and ears...there is so much you miss....Be brave. Trust in these words they will not deceive...Throw away that Mind of man, it is mechanical in a natural World. I give these words to the World, they are not empty...I will take care of all monetary matters...Do not Fear, it blocks progress, it prevents our methods working...we need to see the trust and faith in your heart for all to come true. It is hoped in future Years, that you will be able to look-back, and to help Others who are in need of companionship and sharing.'

KEYPOINTS NI12
a) High Spirit are Aware of all we think and feel.
b) Our attitudes, fear and emotional responses, can restrict our Spiritual progress and also limit our physical benefits.
c) If we accept that we are guided to a better World with the minimum of pain, then although there are Lessons to be learnt along our pathway, it will not be necessary to repeat and suffer the same Lessons again before we make   the correct choices.
d) When Lessons are repeated, they come with increasing severity.
e) To Achieve Spiritual progress your motives need to be genuine.
f) There is an expectation, in due course of Time, that what you personally gain will be used to help Others.

13.24 'We need you both to present to the World, perfect Love and friendship of the purest kind.'

KEYPOINTS NI13
a) The Key to all Life is Love of the purest kind.
b) It is possible to achieve Spiritual Growth by learning to Understand the nature of Others; and by relating this experience to Understanding yourself, your relationships, your feelings, your emotions, and the pure beauty of Nature, and all about you.

13.25 White Eagle continues... 'The gift of the Child to Helana, and the gift of the Holy Ghost are given to reward her achievements, for she has clawed her way from the Darkness to the highest Realms of Spirit...Understand the hardships she has endured by facing the realities of her true nature...this reward can only be given to a few...I am her soul-Carer for the work that is to be achieved...it is as in the Words of the '<u>Book Of Knowledge</u>' and here spoken by your Spirit:... 'John, Helana has the key to unlocking this knowledge...there will be no greater Love and understanding and honesty given to your Spirit by Helana...
She has always been the greatest Love for you on the Earth-plane.'
{*The Book of Knowledge referred to here, is the Book which sets out the Order of Events for this World and for all the other Worlds throughout the Universe*}

13.26 'Understand my dear Man, that when she is prickly and seemingly uncaring, it is not her true nature...it is the influence of Others around her...our Hearts cry out at times...you have not seen the beauty of Helana...Take her to your Heart, completely, unconditionally, knowing the perfect Spirit within...All else is other influences around and within...Why do Others wish to appear to the World as other than gentle Beings?'

~~~~~~

14.15 Judith receives a message from White Eagle who writes... 'Even Guides have Lessons to learn, especially those who have attained only level 5...this situation with Helana was an opportunity for Helana's Guide to learn forgiveness...the Guide will not be changed...It is hoped John that you will ask forgiveness of that Guide for the derogatory way you treated that Being in the previous Life...In this way you can both grow'.

KEYPOINTS N6
a) **Healing of Past Situations is a necessity for Spiritual Growth.**
b) **When in the Spirit World you retain your personality.**
• **Ideally, all those who attain the level of Spirit Guide have progressed sufficiently in the ways of Love, Understanding, Experience and Compassion for any individual historical bitterness to have been put aside.**
• **Very occasionally a Situation can develop when 'emotions' re-surface and conflict can arise.**
• **Fortunately these occurrences are very rare.**
• **Even Guides need to be taught and to learn, not everyone is 'perfect'.**
c) **Your Spirit Guides can be changed to match your Spiritual growth, awareness, and the needs of your Lifetime experience.**

14.16 White Eagle continues........ 'We will now address the question of Helana being totally ruled by her Guide; this is an unusual Problem... Helana has chosen to take no responsibility for her actions; it is therefore difficult for her to make her Mind up on anything...She has closed the door on her own Spiritual progress, for how can she learn if she makes no choices for herself?...Do not hide behind Spirit........It is our fervent wish that you John will gain a higher awareness of Spirit, and Helana will come down and be more Earthly, and somewhere along each of your Journey's, you will meet and find a compatibility that allows the Love between you to flow freely...Helana must not feel she is losing her Spirituality, nor must she feel inadequate in any way...John, you need to lift your Spirit and to give the unconditional Love and understanding being asked of you. All is standing still'

~~~~~~

14.56 On Sunday, 22nd November, I receive the following message via Helana, in trance, from White Eagle.... 'Helana has given so much, and sacrificed so much, neither your Mind, nor your Spirit understands this...It is necessary now to move you along your chosen Pathways... FORWARD CHRISTIAN SOLDIERS, United in what you do, and what you say...I have no greatness around me, only my wisdom and my knowledge... I come to bring you this message, clearly, visibly, so that you will understand the Truth that is to be given...I may not say clearly, in graphic detail what is black and what is white. You have the Mind to understand, your Spirit needs to be awakened to do the work...You need to find yourself within John, to gain the understanding, in this way your Spirit will grow again to the wonderful Spirit which we see buried in the depths of the Earth... So much has been gained by you with Helana, but so much has been lost! We cannot allow this to continue. Helana is needed in this Land to bring Love to the Hearts of many.'

14.57 'It is time for you John to move on...You have been given the best of her knowledge, you have seen the tears. She cries for trees, animals etc...she cradles the World like a baby, but her own Heart is deprived. How can she heal the World when her own Heart is torn apart? Many lessons have been learnt in your time together. The Love will not end, it will not be forgotten. It has healed the very Heart that lies within. We cannot say how much has been given, but believe John, you have had the Love of many from one...We cannot say, at this time, what is to be...but it will be given in your sleep, for your Spirit to understand, and hopefully to leave this Child in peace. You do not Understand how the Spirit within can behave differently to the human Being...Helana will not remember this message...If only you could lift up your Spirit...there is a wealth of knowledge to be shared with the World...You have been given so much knowledge; the vision of this Child, her very nature, is all that you needed to see, as to what is needed in your daily Life...

We do not give up hope, we need you to work for Spirit, we need your strength and character, we need the gentleness, the Understanding, the listening, to fulfill that which you can achieve in this Lifetime. We are lost for words as to what to say to help you to understand fully what is being said...Look at the pattern of your Life...the Journeys traveled, this will give some Understanding'.

14.58 'All is as It should be, All will continue. Rest your head tonight, Knowledge and Understanding will be given. We can do no more, we hope and pray you will understand fully and allow your Spirit to be free.
Have peace in your Heart, that all is as it should be, always. 'Reach out for the Light John. Be free, do not allow these human feelings to hold you back. Put together the Lessons of the past few days in your Mind, so that your Spirit will understand. You are as two Minds!, allow your Mind to teach your Spirit.'

KEYPOINT N18
All our Life is planned; all is arranged by High Spirit.
{I did not fully grasp at the time, the significance of this message, or the implications. The problem quite simply was that it subsequently took me 18 months to get around to re-reading this message, by which time of course all was History! When you are living in a situation and hoping that all can be healed so long as you apply yourself enough, then your Mind deals with and copes with the daily emotional interaction, and the pressures of Life are sufficient to pre-occupy yourself. This Message implies that Helana and I were brought together simply for me to achieve the level of understanding and Spiritual Awareness necessary, Spirit have decided that my rate of progress has been insufficient, Helana's Spirit is unhappy.
I can learn no more from her, so I am being told that THE END is nigh! emotions, and human feelings, do not seem to matter, do they?}

14.66 It is Thursday, 26th November, White Eagle writes through Helana........
'My dear Man, these words will perhaps help you to understand the ways of Nature. I write for you this day in the hope that your pain and suffering may be eased. The words of a song so clear in the Mind of Helana is one from a revealing Story of Life on the Ocean ship Titanic. The two Lovers who met on board this vessel were briefly meant to be together for a short time only, their Love was truly found.

Pure, unconditional Love was found for such a short time in the lives of these people, but all Love that can be found in the Hearts of these People and many Others, matters not for the shortness of time it is held in their Hearts. The Spirits live on my dear Man.

The Spirits are free to travel to loved-Ones, as you are aware, at any time of the Day or Night, my Dear, your Spirits can be together in Love and Friendship. Jealousy my dear Man, has no place in the Heart of Man, it causes pain and suffering of a deep kind. All Love is shared, as you Love, so do all of those around you, and they in turn Love, all who are around them, and so the ripples grow.
Your Love has been found for the time needed. As the Spirits on the Ocean waves, they are not apart to this day, their Love lives on my dear Man.
The song relates this so clearly, for you are aware of your father's Spirit when he chooses to visit you and to bring you Love, Healing and Strength, so can you not then understand that the Love of Helana cannot ever end, for her Spirit has loved you so dearly over many Lifetimes'.

14.67 'In each Lifetime she has tried to show you the beautiful ways of Nature, but to no account. It is hoped that you will retain all that has been given by her Spirit, and her true ways, to help you continue in your Spiritual Awareness. All that can be given, has now been given, and time now is left for you to decide which way you wish to stay...in the life of beauty, or hidden Underground. The choice is yours my dear Man......... Do you not see Helana's Life is like that of a child, the child is a gift from GOD, the child is then released and given to the World and its Peoples, to bring Love to their own Lives. In giving the child in this way, you are healing and giving Love to the World. As you give you receive. To release the Child in this Way, it is as GOD gave to you, you give in return and so the Love goes on. We bring to you this understanding my dear Man, in the hope that your Heart will understand and be healed. You will not be apart, for the Hearts do indeed live on always. It is only the bodies, the physical my dear Man which are apart. Do not we ask be so upset, for you have, and will continue to Love in the truest way. You are, do not forget, Spiritual Beings on Earth.'

KEYPOINTS N21
```
a) Spiritual Love never dies, once achieved.
b) The duration of the physical time, when Love has been
achieved, that you remain together on the Earth-Plane,
is not significant.
```

14.82 White Eagle writes, and this Text is also greatly reduced:......................
'The pains within Helana's arms, feet and body are felt like needles protruding into her very Life.......we remind you again that 'Love can only be found in Freedom'.

Lose your selfish ways, allow her her freedom, and Love will blossom like the flowers on a Tree in May. Do you not see the disease; which is so often in our Garden of Eden, appearing on the leaves from all the pain and sorrow harbored by the Minds of many around them. Beauty is being strangled by possessive and selfish needs.

Do not be selfish in your ways, for the World is in need. Count your blessings my dear Man, for Others may not get this chance...you cannot own a Person or Love...All is shared in Spirit...she has given her all, almost her life. The help given must now end, for the sap of this beautiful Tree is in need of replenishing with the Love that is intended.'
'All Situations given in Life are given for your Spiritual Understanding... We bring to you all the hurdles you must face, so that you can knock them down one-by-one, and so be able to walk away freely with no obstacles in your Way.'

~~~~~~

15.03 A new Guide is to be brought to you.
White Eagle writes; 'You, John, can now choose your own way of becoming and being Spiritual. We expect all of our Helpers and all true Believers to walk the Earth as of the Earth, but never forgetting that within they carry and host a beautiful Spirit...Do not be too flippant, especially as now your commitment has been fully accepted by us. Spirituality should also be happy, for without laughter your World would be even darker. All help will be given to assist with your Earthly happenings...It is beholden for you to ensure that within your capabilities; that you do what you are asked to, to the best of your abilities. Have faith; that no Other can take the place that has been allocated to you.'

15.40 On December 24th, I am told 'All knowledge is within you John, you do not need to read, you only need to ask. We appreciate that reading stimulates the questions in your Mind so it is useful from that point of view.'
We attend the Church of Ireland, BallyHolme, the Christmas Eve Service, in Bangor. Jesus stands next to us. Earlier, Helana has felt 'kicking' inside her womb. We return home and at 01.20 on the 25th, the following message is then delivered by Helana:
'A Meeting has been called to present to you, John, the facts of all that there is to Be, has Been, and will Be. I am White Eagle...I bring to you these words this day...You have knowledge of who I am. This is a trust within your Heart my dear Man. No other brings to you a message this day. I give you my sign; therefore release this child from the disbelief of the words that pass her lips on many occasions...I do not come with ease this time, for there is pain in my Heart for the World, and its needs are so great at this Time.'

'I have requested that my presence should be with this Lady, for there is a great deal to be achieved...I am stern of face. I do not wish to take away the splendour of this day on the Earth-Plane. I share the mind, the body, not quite the voice of this lady, but no words will enter within.'

15.41 White Eagle continues...
'Upon this night there was a child born within our History of Mankind. (not the true day!) the Child is born to Mary, the mother of this child, so gentle, so wise. We were saddened by your lack of listening to the Priest 'Alan', his words were so profound, we will bring you the meaning... the mother Mary was unmarried, young, 16-18 years, to be told that a child would be given! Can you imagine the confusion of this child, she was engaged to Joseph, can you imagine the shame?...it is not my child! Nevertheless, the trust was there from Mary. Was it me? or was it the word of GOD?
They decided to listen and to follow the Instructions that were given. We ask you to understand the shear trust of the mother...to listen, to hear the words spoken, by no-one she could see or touch...But she followed every step obediently...
You do not see, you pull...you trust because you feel the 'tug'. As with Mary and Joseph, they still had no concrete evidence, however, at the birth of Jesus there were animals and wise-Men with gifts. This was the 'tug', it was proof that the child was truly the Messiah and all was as it should be...All through the child's life these little 'tugs' existed......'

15.42 'If you do not still your Mind John, you miss so many 'tugs'. Try harder to slowdown the Mind, bring peace to your Mind; Observe all about you, Concentrate your Mind. Find the complete Understanding, of what we try to say, to help, and to guide you. In writing also, ensure your Mind does not wander, for if it does you do not write accurately. We say at this time, there is only so much time to gain the necessary commitment. We are eager to move you all on your way, but there are things needed to enable this to happen. TRY HARDER my dear Man. It is necessary if you wish to become a part of this Lady. It cannot happen if you insist on living your Life as it has been........
We remind you again about the kitten, have you looked behind this story relating to Helana? All is given for you to understand, to grow, to progress. The man Philip is in the Past. Take care my dear Man that this does not happen to you!...We remind you again, for these words will not be given again. BE AT PEACE!... Please, we ask you to understand all that has been given...Do not file away the papers. The Events of the past few Days are vitally important.'

KEYPOINTS DP11
a) Messages from Spirit are often disguised in the form of visions, dreams or incidents, which if we are not observant and aware, we will miss.
b) It is necessary to question every happening as to its significance. White Eagle calls these Events 'Tugs'.
c) A still Mind, at peace, is essential to become capable of receiving true messages.

15.52 'We feel for the time your Lady is absent from your Day, in the future Days to come, a thought on how your thoughts and actions; can and do affect the Lives of Others, and how much in this Life has changed from that of your past-Lives, to change what has become part of your true Nature.'

KEYPOINTS DP13
a) Thoughts on the Earth help to create our Future World and experiences.
b) Thoughts in Spirit World act to create the Present.

15.53 'You are all born with an element of GOD within you, to reach the very Heart and existence of Mankind, but there are many barriers that block this wonderful fulfillment from happening...
Too often we see failure within Man's Mind for the fear of retribution, but all is in the Hands of GOD, for as he sees the Sins of the Past and works towards repenting of these, GOD's Love upholds you and helps and guides those who seek this golden Pathway'.

15.54 'We feel at this present time my dear Man, your Heart is in need of Learning, and bring to you this message this Day to help and guide you along your chosen Pathway. We feel your anger and pain many times my dear Man, but we ask you to understand that we are here only to help and to guide you. Go with Peace in your Heart my dear Man and know that we are beside you, waiting for your true Light to shine through the Darkness felt within your Mind at this present time. White Eagle writes for you this Day my dear Man, a trusted name within your Mind'.

15.97 I receive a strong message from White Eagle, via Judith, the Key Points made are:
- I need to delve into and question more the messages I receive
- I need to speak less and behave less like GOD!
- The Child will not be brought in this Lifetime
- Helana does not need to be physically with me for the work to continue, her thoughts and actions are not Love
- I need to find the Person within me, know myself, love myself as I am, appreciate my own self-worth.

- I am not to feel that I am good enough for any woman on the Earth!
- I am not to rely upon anyone else for my happiness
- I am not above reproach
- I am not to blame Others for my faults
- I am to find empathy and compassion for Others
- I am to repair the damage to Other more gentle Spirits
- I am to rectify the damage I have done to so many Others in so many Lifetimes
- Acknowledge my True Feelings for Constance and heal her Spirit. (she regrets she cannot live with me and draws near with love)

~~~~~~

A1.42 'Helana my Dear you have said the words, but your Heart has not always been present...Do not let John take away your true nature, for you also have a Life to lead...he will see in time the need for you to have your Freedom...do not despair that you are not progressing...he has a wealth of knowledge in his Spirit which he will soon become aware of...he will then pull you forwards with him. There are many things left unsaid, you need now to ask John what his true feelings are.........'

KEYPOINTS HS15
a) **In so much as Trees also have Spirits it is possible for some Beings to tune-in to their energy levels...In particular Helana's Origins were from a Green Planet where Trees were respected and an integral Part of the Existence; Helana can communicate with Trees.**
b) **It is useful to visualize a corridor of Trees when one wishes to Meditate and to calm One's-Self.**
c) **Whenever you travel or walk close to Trees, feel the vibrations emanating, particularly from the older Trees.**

A1.43 'Do not worry about your Man while he is away at the weekend, this time will be useful for your understanding and will show his true feelings of Love for you. You need to learn trust for your Man also, he will not be unfaithful...<u>Do not tempt anyone else into your Heart my Dear, we do not see this as a Problem, but something you need to be aware of... Do not forget that temptation still plays a part, for from the origins of Life come these Traits which need to be overcome by so many</u>...your Man has learnt many lessons from past Relationships and is fully aware of the dangers here.
He will not walk away from you unless you damage his faith and trust...each or both of you have had infidelity in your previous Lives, we need now for you to break these chains...Walk away my Dear Helana from temptation and your Man will do the same...do not allow one moment to destroy all that you have.....'

A1.44 'Do not forget the forbidden fruit!!...you need to find complete trust and faith in each Other and your honest actions, so that no Man or Woman can put asunder what marriage has taken place and will remain always my Dear...Do not fear these words, but we felt it necessary to bring these to your Attention.....Go now with peace in your Heart and allow your Lives to flow, as do the rivers of Life.'
{note well this message!}

A1.45 On Saturday, 26th September
'Your beginnings my Dear, account for no more memories or darkness to prevail or indeed to prevent you from progressing...forget all that has passed, for you have moved forwards so fast my Dear that all has been left behind and we have removed all past Darkness, so that we can bring to you only Light of a true kind. Do not doubt these Words, or your own understanding.'
KEYPOINT HS16
It is possible for the memories held within our Spirits to be removed or dimmed.

A1.46 'Your Man John will now progress rapidly, as all Past for him also has been left behind, and only a few short moments be ahead of him now to regain all that has been lost. The past Ladies in his Life-time will cease to become the problem you have encountered, for all past memories of your Beginnings have been taken away from their Minds and consciousness. Their Spirits also have been dimmed accordingly to allow you both the freedom now you so deserve. Your Man has worked well my Dear and it remains now only for the Mind to release the barriers that have been created by time.'

A1.47 On Sunday 27th September 1998
'.All has been achieved.......We see a marked Improvement in the Man's Mind now that a more settled Spirit resides within the Man's Being. {our Spirits are joined as One}...
Do not doubt his fears my Dear for they are real.....his fears of losing you are greatly heightened...we see a little concern, for you realize the possessive nature of this man.... Understanding will be gained in time of the merits of Freedom...your work will continue with this Man for some time until his Lessons have been learnt, for his Mind to let go of all that holds him back.

The Spirit is gentle my Dear and comes to you now with the fullness of Love everlasting. Your Bodies will unite this evening and the closeness felt will be wonderful for you both to experience. Do not fear this my Dear for as you are now of the one Spirit, what is good for the Goose is also good for the Gander.......Communication will commence first from Touch..... then true Conversation will follow after a short time............it is to be truly a magical time for you both'. {this refers to the Mind-Thought link}

```
KEYPOINTS HS17
There is a clear indication that Helana is with me for
the purpose of teaching me; and also that when this
teaching is completed then she will then decide whether
to depart! {This follows on from the Lessons brought to
me by Constance!...}
Separate to the teaching of John, Helana has been told
that there is a quite separate special purpose for her
Life ahead.
```

A1.48 On Monday 28th September 1998
'...Your Understanding and Love for this Man has always been wonderful for us to see...we see now your commitment to one another will not end in this Life-time... you are from one source my Dear, one GOD, one Being, you are forever returned to the source from whence you come. All Beings are from one source.... From wherever their Lives take place, they will always return to the one source of Life and here in Spirit we see only the Spirit...Do not fear your origins, for it makes no difference my Dear to us here in Spirit...All is Love...Love is Life and your deep Love for this planet Earth will never cease...for you my Dear have helped to create the very Life there is to be found on this Earth.'

```
KEYPOINT HS18
Both Helana and I originated on different Planets and
from different Life Forms. When the Earth Experiment
commenced we were brought together in the Human Life
Form...as some of the Characters recorded in the Bible
Book, Genesis.
```

A1.49 On Tuesday, 29th September 1998
'...Your smile is welcomed my Dear, and your Spirit recognizes the need for this. So many times your happiness is dashed by this Man. My Dear, Do you feel you can continue in this way for a while longer?.
Do not give-up on this Man for his Understanding is so close and his Spirit is raised sufficiently now to allow his true nature to rise to the forefront of his Mind.'

A1.50 'The World's needs are fully known to your Spirit. Your Spirit cries out for the peace that is needed my Dear. The wondrous Mind is not fully aware as yet as to what these Needs are...but understand blocking occurs from the Spirit of the Man as he learns yet again to share your Love with the World. Do not allow him to prevent you from doing this...you have a need, it is your work and your true nature my Dear... you have moved from the darkness, now only Light prevails, for your Spirit is aware of the sadness caused by Darkness of any kind...

Your Man has returned to the grave of his loved-One, who now resides within him. Your Spirits have now concluded this Lifetime....it was necessary for the Tears to flow.

{I was asked to visit Over-Worton once more, to say goodbye to this Lifetime as Richard and Catherine...see Past Lives}

KEYPOINTS HS19
a) The greater Purpose is hinted at, and referred to, on several occasions.
b) The Spirit and the Mind have separate identities.
c) The Spirit can and does override and influence our own thoughts and actions, but also those of others.

A1.51 KEYPOINTS HS20
a) Spiritual Awareness and progress will be restricted by 'unfinished business' from previous Lifetimes.
b) It may be necessary to re-visit these Lifetimes to release the 'Cycle of Hate' which may be trapped, such that the sequence of Events is repeated and repeated in subsequent Lifetimes until true healing occurs.
c) Not only do these Cycles restrict you own individual Spiritual growth, but they also impinge on Others in your Peer-Group et al. *{see Chapter on Spiritual Awareness}*

A1.52 'It is very important for you to be seen...you are protected at all times. Without your presence on the Earth-Plane all would fail...a return to your Host-Planet, or anywhere else, is not expected by us upon your return to Spirit.......the choice will be yours and this will be honoured..
A human Being has surrounded your Spirit for many Life-Times........you will be given the choice of whether you wish to return to your Host-Planet,
or to Reside in Spirit as an Angel,
or to Return to the Earth-Plane,
or a Life of more Understanding to your Mind.
Your Mind we feel has already decided and we ask you now to consider carefully the full implications of this Decision.'

KEYPOINT HS21
We choose our Lives and the experiences our SOUL needs, before we are born, we are of course guided into this choice, or indeed some need to be pushed!

A1.53 'We wish to clarify that a decision to return to help the cause on the Earth-Plane, would not result in a Lifetime similar to your previous ones of struggle and torment. All that you have gained in this Lifetime will not be lost and will be achieved at an earlier stage in your development from child to adulthood...believe these words my Dear, they are needed for your peace of Mind...White Eagle writes with you my Dear...every word has true meaning my Dear.'
'I am honoured to be part of this and honoured to be by your side at all times. Walk the Earth my Dear with Light in your footsteps that will guide you along the heavenly way. Let wings be on your feet my Dear, for you will truly fly.'

A1.54 On 7th October 1998
'Go with our blessings my Dear and know that you are always in our tender, loving care, at all times...your safety is our main concern and that of the child within...do not doubt all is well my Dear and peace will reign within your beloved Land. Let our Hearts be filled with joy for smiles we need to see upon the face of our beloved One, so beautiful and full of grace. Rest in our Hearts my Dear as we see the flower of the Earth-Plane bloom once more, more fully than ever before. Let your Tears be the mountain rain, pure and refreshing, cleansing the very Earth they fall upon...your Man awaits his Spirit my Dear, and when this Day arrives, all will be beautiful. DO NOT, PLEASE WE PRAY, GIVE-UP ON THIS MAN.'

A1.55 On 8th October 1998
My Dear do understand that all that is given will be given. Your needs are for both Inner Warmth and for Spiritual Warmth...Do not be harassed by this Man or by any other Spirit...We will guide you in any decision you make...the Rose Petals that you now walk upon will always be given.
We fear (*respect*) your words my Dear, and your Thoughts, and we will stand by these remember always... ...the Spirit of the Man stands by awaiting this re-union with the Man. His Mind is frozen like the Heart my Dear, but we feel sure you will find a way to melt away again this frozen mass which surrounds and hides the Man's true nature.
Go now with our Blessings my Dear and purchase the winter Coat that you feel you need to.'

A4.30 The Words from White Eagle are particularly harsh...
'The pains in Helana's arms, feet and body are felt like needles protruding into her very Life-force. This is also caused by an 'Ivy-like Being' entwined around her, taking away the Life-force which is within her. It is not only you my dear Man that causes these pains, but your ways are a major contribution to this fact.
We remind you again. 'LOVE CAN ONLY BE FOUND IN FREEDOM'. Lose your Selfish Ways, allow her her Freedom, and Love will blossom like the flowers on a Tree in May, when my dear Man, you care to recall that this child of Life was born.

Do you not see how like Nature you are? All of you are as a Tree. How then do you see yourself my dear Man? What kind of Tree do you think we see here in Spirit when we look at the Man, John at this Time. Do you see Flowers or Buds forming?
Do you see disease which is so often in our Garden of Eden, appearing on the Leaves now from the Pain and Sorrow harboured by the Minds of Many? Beauty being strangled by possessive and selfish Needs...............'

A4.31 The task you have undertaken is not an easy One. Self analysis and criticism is never easy. *{Since I personally embarked upon this Learning process, I hope that I have become a more Loving, more Caring, more Compassionate Individual. Only Others who know you can enlighten you to the Truth, certainly your Guides will not hesitate to correct your Manner should it be lacking in any direction}*.

- You need to Give before you can Receive, this is not a Selfish journey.
- You need to Heal your Relationships if this is possible.
- Give Love to receive Love. Give loving Thoughts and Prayers to those around you who are awkward or bitter. Show them by your actions and attitude that you care. Love is the most powerful prime mover in the Universe.
- Even the hardest of People will cry if the right Chord is touched. I have never cried so much since I embarked upon this Journey. Do not be afraid to let Others see you Cry, they too have their Lessons to learn.
- Help Any One, any Thing, or any Creature in distress.
- Think positive. Think Spiritual. Feel Compassion.
- What is the purpose for this Experience?
- What can I or Others learn from this? Why have I met this Person?
- Respect Others for their Views. Do not be bigoted. Do not become a Bore.

A4.32 Everyone has Talents, everyone can Contribute to Save the Planet and Nature... Picture a Scale, a Balance.
a) The whole of the FUTURE of EVERY PERSON, EVERY CHILD, EVERY CREATURE, EVERY ANIMAL, EVERYTHING YOU CARE FOR is finely Balanced.
b) EVERYONE who spreads Light and Unselfish Love makes a contribution to saving our Planet. There could be 3 Billion People who are Promoting Love, there could be 3 Billion People sitting on the Fence, there could be 3 Billion People spreading Evil. It only takes ONE PERSON to make a difference, to walk across the Pendulum from Darkness to Light, to jump down from the Fence and to make a positive Contribution, to cause the Whole Pendulum to swing towards Love.

- *Is that person YOU?... Will YOU make the difference?....What different will YOU DO TOMORROW?*

CONSIDER a Nuclear BOMB, a Critical Mass is necessary to cause an Explosion. Up to the point of reaching the final Critical Mass there is little change, then all at once a huge release of Energy is created.

Relate this now to our World. When sufficient People with Light and Love exist, an Explosion of Love will occur. HEAVEN on EARTH will become a Reality. We will have secured our Planet for the Future, there will occur a massive Energy Shift and the Whole will be transformed. This is the Objective, to eliminate Evil.

- <u>YOUR actions NOW could make the difference for TOMORROW</u>.

```
{this completes the section of messages received from
White Eagle, up to March 1999; to ascertain the actual
time sequence and context, it will be necessary to
purchase the Book Of Truth and Knowledge, to be
published in June 2002.}
```

end of messages

##

messages from JESUS

[Throughout the Book, Jesus features as a Friend and Guide to both Helana and John,
It is necessary to read and ponder the BOOK OF TRUTH AND KNOWLEDGE to gain an understanding of the special relationship between the Three. Many words were given by Jesus, Mary, Isaiah, Joshua and Others in the first few Days of the initial Meeting between Helana and John; none of these were recorded by John; indeed they would probably make a Book themselves. The first week of the Relationship was critical, to persuade John to walk away from Lorna, and to build a new Life with Helana for the greater Purpose which he was not aware of at that time.
ALL is remembered by Spirit, so when John has achieved his full SPIRITUAL AWARENESS, it is hoped to be able to recall these times to their fullest extent

6.05 On Friday, 5th June, at 00.30 hrs, it is my Birthday, and Greetings are received from Spirit, a beautiful Card from Helana, and a Present. We are asked to move forwards and to forget the Past. We have been chosen to carry out the Work necessary in Ireland........a beautiful Land of Mountains, Lakes, Rivers, Trees and Hills.......so I am told:

'Helana's love for you will not falter, She has given you her All; her Heart, her Love, her Spirit, her Mind and her Being. She has climbed mountains and overcome many obstacles to be by your side. It has been a struggle and she has shed many tears. Her beautiful eyes have seen much sadness and loneliness, but now we can see happiness and Love of a true Kind.
No Other can fulfill your needs in the same way. Support her in every way, do not falter, do not flirt with Others. Do not underestimate the depth of her Love for you, nor her beautiful nature. She is a child of Nature, and yours to treasure for the rest of your Life.
Her Love protects you, wherever you are, her Thoughts are never far away from you. You share such closeness and beautiful Love; this is exactly what the child needs so that it can grow in Love of a true Kind, and find Understanding of its place in the Universe.
Without this new purpose in your Life, John, it would have ended in tears and grief. You have been brought together for the special needs of the World and its People. You have both discovered the Love needed at the same time. All is as it should be, the healing process has begun; your Lives will now be entwined together for eternity, by a Bond so strong that it cannot be broken; nothing can come between you. ONLY your individual Free-wills can change this.'

6.06 'Spirit give to you today, the gift of your Spirits coming together for all Time. The feelings within are a preparation for this Day. You will know immediately that Helana's Spirit is within you from the beautiful feeling of warmth, Love and peace inside your Body. Peace is synonymous with true Love........There cannot be anything more wonderful than when your Spirits entwine for the first time. You John, will be unaware of the greatness of this moment until a future Time when peace can be found. You have shared many Lives together, but your Spirits have remained separate but within. Once entwined you can never be separated. On another Day you will be entwined at an Earthly level.'

KEYPOINTS TP4
a) Spirit talk of two levels of Love, the typical human level is mainly of a sexual nature and is not considered to represent true Love in any way.
b) Spirit say FRIENDSHIP is a better indication of true Love.
The most powerful Bond is when the SOULS entwine, for then we achieve a completeness of Spirit, Mind and Body which will LAST FOREVER, through every existence.

d) Whether subsequently the Bodies are together is not that important, for the Souls can unite whenever they wish to, every night in our sleep for example.
e) A beautiful feeling within your Body, of warmth and peace will be evidence of the presence of Spirit coming to you in true Love.

6.07 'There are special Times ahead, reach out, bring to Helana the glory of your Love, let her see the Spirit in your eyes, raise yourself to her level. Do this, and Helana's Love will be complete; this will enable Helana's Spirit to advance and to help Others. These Words come from true Spirit, we sit by Helana's Side and have no doubt that you John, will succeed.
You John are the Spokesman, the Letter-writer, the Messenger, the Bringer of healing to those in need. Your frivolous nature amuses us. Do not lose this, as a lightness of Spirit is sometimes necessary to put across the message. It makes Helana smile, she has laughter in her eyes and smile. We thank you John for bringing Helana into the true Light of Happiness, and true Love. Peace be with you both, allow us to take your words; strive for what is good and beautiful. Go now with peace in your Heart, all is to be beautiful.
We wish you again a Happy Birthday and the gift of Love is yours.'

6.08 'Helana will have a tough time ahead, Many will wish her unbeautiful things, blame and darkness of Thoughts; be it family or friends, dismiss them as friends of the Past. A wealth of knowledge is to be gained from the Hook Norton experience. Let this experience pass, it is their loss.' (this concerned the presence of a dark Spirit called 'Dan', who was becoming a threat to the children living at the House. Jesus had requested us to visit the Property and to clear it of this Ghost from the Past. It was necessary to follow a special procedure to achieve this, but the folks living there were dismissive, unbelieving and rude, so the exorcism by us never took place.)

6.09 I am given a coughing fit for drinking too much wine! July 17th is given as the date for us to go to Ireland. I am to explore the possibility of a transfer within my Organization to their Northern Ireland office. We are to consider an immediate move from Aylesbury to another location near to Enstone. Helana's feet are tapping rapidly, a sign of progress, and the need to move-on. {Aylesbury and Banbury are both poor locations for Spirit Reception}
KEYPOINT TP5
Certain Locations are poor for Spirit communication. This has been caused by their dark History; which has created a covering negative shadow and shield to the Light, and so blocks and restricts the ease of communication.

6.10 At 12 Mid-night. A message is received from Jesus, He is pleased with our progress. There is to be no turning back. I feel my Spirit raised within me. Jesus speaks through Helana:
'Helana is crying, sobbing profusely, in need of your strength John. This is a sad day for her, You have no idea of how great is her Spirit, and how it suffers and bears pain for so Many and still protects you. We struggle with our words, for Helana does not wish us to inform you John, of the conflict within her. However, you need to gain an Understanding. Be re-assured there is no need for jealousy.'

6.11 'The tears shed by Helana are for the Spirit of Jack. It is the parting of the ways, they were born as twins and they remain as twins; with the entwining of your Spirit, John, with Helana's, this is no longer possible. They will remain as brother and sister, but there is to be no more physical contact in this Lifetime. Jack's Spirit knows this.'

6.12 'You John, will now begin to feel the pain and suffering and other emotions which Helana feels. The Love shared between you will bring to you all the healing which is necessary at this time. There is a great deal to be achieved in the next few Days; not only in your daily living, but also in your sleeping hours. Strength will be given and rest assured. You will be protected at all times. Helana will need your support and tenderness at all times, but especially at this time.'
KEYPOINT TP6
When the Spirits are entwined, the Human emotions are shared also.

6.13 'Your work for Spirit has begun. Your work is to be shared with Helana and with Judith. A greatness of achievement will be obtained in this Lifetime; your work together will create a Community and a History. It is for this reason you have been brought together, and the presence of Helana in your Life has enabled this to be.'

6.14 'Go now in peace, with calm and serenity at your side. You are to be placed in the Land called Ireland to perform certain tasks, these will be given when needed. You will be guided in every way. Remember, Helana is a fragile flower, but, so strong.......there are many things you must learn and understand, but all will be given'......Helana sighs and I feel the sigh within me.

6.15 Helana is given a vision of the Book of Life, in Blue with Gold writing. This book for-tells the future of the Universe, and is also mentioned in the New Testament.(John)

KEYPOINTS TP7

a) There exists a Book of Life which outlines the future of our Universe, and which is used as a reference to all significant happenings.
b) Your Spirit 'flips' when it recognizes Spirits that it has known previously; in previous Lives. Spirit recognition occurs throughout our Lives. Our eyes change when this occurs.
c) Everyone needs to be very careful not to confuse Spirit recognition with human emotional feelings. Many relationships fail because of confusion in our Minds.
d) Spirit Love can confuse and affect human feelings, your relationships and your perception of Others.
e) Our Spirits always search for PERFECT love. Our Partner should be right for us in every respect. If we find that we have made a wrong choice, we should leave that relationship, and continue to search for true love.
f) Without SPIRITUAL AWARENESS it is impossible for us to know that we have made a correct choice. All that one can do, is to learn to know Oneself.
g) Forgive yourself for previous relationships that have failed. Learn from your previous relationships.

{I need to review my past Life, to forgive myself. This is the key to Spiritual progression. Everyone is searching, Everyone is doing the same........In previous Lives I have been Helana's Child. Jack has been our Child.}

6.16 It is 7th June, at 00.30 hrs. A message is received from Jesus. 'My dear Ones, do not forget who I am, in many ways you think of me as the Great-One. But I was just a Man. Do not forget also that you have the strength and the power within your Spirit to perform the miracles which were performed in my Lifetime on this Earth-plane.
I have seen many Lives come and go, but none so great as this One. You have traveled far my dear Ones. The time has come to bring you together in a way that will last for Eternity. We have asked you John, many times to confirm:
(a) Do you wish to share your Heart with Helana?.....my answer 'I give her my Lifetime.'
(b) Do you wish to change your Mind?....my answer is 'No'
Jesus continues: 'Helana has made the same choices, in this way the coming together of both your Spirits will be...Slowly you will feel the presence of each Other within...John, take the same position as Helana. *{this refers to the way I was sitting}* .

The bells are ringing in Heaven.....A purity of Heart and Mind will exist between you...Share not your Bodies with Another. Imaginary Rings are placed upon our Fingers,....Helana first....Your Families are present with us today in Spirit to witness this Ceremony....The Child will not be born out of Wedlock....A meal is prepared for you...Helana can see this...the Fruit represents your Labours.....the Gates of Heaven are now open to you Both.....indeed it will be Paradise! Together you will reside in Spirit and on the Earth...I, Jesus, will always remain by your Side...Take our Love, and the Light of true Spirit who bring to you these words of Truth, Wisdom and Understanding....May your Hearts rejoice with the Love that is found, as Ours do on this Day.....Sleep easy now, with your Minds at peace.......All is as it should be.'

6.17 'You John, are trying to prove something to yourself; this is not necessary. You have a choice to make. How much easier would your life be, if it was not one of providing for Others. Let go the Guilt...the pressure for you to work the way that you do will be considerably reduced. With pressure such as this, what chance have you to relax? It is not possible.
{I have been paying maintenance of £ 300- £700 per month for many years.}
To alter your situation will cause a great deal of animosity. Your Mother will have a great deal to say, Helana will be blamed. This is not emotional blackmail. We cannot say stop working! But, if you change your Lifestyle, then you will not be surrounded by people who take and give nothing. You have the capability of loving perfectly, for loving sake...not for reward. You could choose to continue your work as a source of Introductions; you need to use your initiative to solve these problems'.

KEYPOINTS TP8
a) **As you Give, so you shall Receive**
b) **You always have the choice of changing your Lifestyle. It is not necessary, nor desirable, nor intended, that you sacrifice your own Life totally for the benefit of Others. You must also have a quality of Life, so that you can pursue your own Objectives.**
c) **Spirit will not do everything for you, only by your own struggles, your own efforts, and your own suffering, do you learn and retain the value of the Lessons.**

6.18 'See your Life John, as it truly is. Spend as much time as you can dealing with the guilt within your Head. There is always more than one-side to any situation, No-one does anything without a reason, even though they may not be aware of what that reason is. Take-off your Blinkers, you also have the right to live your Life.'

KEYPOINT TP9
No-one does ANYTHING without a reason, even though they may not be aware of that reason in their conscious Mind when the event occurs.

6.19 'Do your utmost to ensure that each of your children realizes how much that you Love them. Have no favorites, they are all Individuals. Your Mother has the deepest of feelings for you, it is sad that she cannot convey this to you. She has not always approved of your Lifestyle'

KEYPOINT TP10
Not everyone has the character or capability of demonstrating their true feelings. This is so sad, for sometimes opportunities are missed and misunderstandings occur which can live with us throughout our Lives and can affect all of our feelings and relationships. *{this message refers not only to my Mother, but also to the man Bryan who took his own Life through a failure to express his true Feelings for Helana}*

6.20 Jesus continues: 'You John, must slow down your pace of Life. Slow down your hands, your mind, your car. A decision will be taken in Ireland. You must demonstrate a willingness to accept the slower pace of Life. Do you love Helana enough? You must follow her guidance and have trust and faith in her. There is no need for jealousy or anger. Accept the moment, leave behind the Past and everything you have previously known. Are you prepared to accept the new Life, and trust in Spirit?

KEYPOINTS TP11
a) Should you wish to live a Spiritual Life, it may be necessary to change the pace of your Lifestyle to one which is more in tune with Spiritual requirements, additionally it will be necessary to lose the Guilt, to heal, and then to leave behind the Past.
b) You cannot walk forwards and still drag with you all the baggage of emotion and feelings from your past Life. How can you form new relationships while you are still injured by the old Ones. You will always keep the Love, the memories, and the good Times; but when you decide to 'Move-On'; it is necessary to break with the Past, however painful this may seem to be at the time.
{IF, the Past is serving only to restrict your progress. remember what you do affects all those about you and in your Peer Group}

c) The Past has brought YOU to the Present, without the Past experiences, YOU would not have the ability, nor the motivation, nor the opportunity to move-on. Be thankful and grateful to those who have brought you to this decision. ALL IS FOR LEARNING!

6.21 On 11th June, Jesus writes: 'A time and a place has been found; you will find the joy of living within this time and place. You have discovered many things this day, the closeness between you both has been found satisfactory to both you, and to Spirit. It has taken many tears, but we feel these have not been wasted. The oceans of your Lives will now start to fill with fishes, the nourishment of Life and calmer waters. Dreams will be found in this Land of Ireland. Think now towards your future and all will be blessed. We have realized in Spirit the true nature of your Souls, and for this reason will allow you to continue. There will be no parting of the waves unless you allow it to happen. Find peace; let our guidance guide you safely on your Journey. You will always remain in the Light and Love of True Spirit. Take the hand John of this lady, many times, and allow her to guide you safely. Go in peace now'

KEYPOINT TP12
High Spirit continually monitor your thoughts, feelings, actions, and objectives. All are taken into account before any chosen pathway can be successfully followed.

6.22 'I, Jesus, am here with you, to help you make the right choices...the World is in need. You John, have a special relationship to Helana who washed my feet when I was on the Cross. She helped me with my suffering when it was needed; now, I am here in Spirit World, and she on the Earth-Plane acts on my behalf.'
(Helana was Rebecca who washed Jesus's feet)

KEYPOINT TP13
Jesus is confirming that our Souls live many Lives, and that nothing we do is ever forgotten.

6.56 On 20th June, at 02.00hrs, a message is delivered from Jesus: 'Be patient John with Brian and Ford, both are Spiritual and receptive, but they do not understand. Helana has seen what they need in terms of Love and Understanding. Allow her to guide and to help these children. Listen to her words. Rome was not built in a day. You are soon to discover in your awareness many things: Who and what you are, and where you are to be. It is to be a time of revelation. Many things have been said which you do not understand fully, but you are aware of the need for and importance of your presence in Northern Ireland at this time. So many are in need. We are all one family, all is shared. The Creator of the one family is GOD in Heaven. There is so much that you do not understand at the present time. Allow yourself to be free. Allow the knowledge of who you are to bring about an Understanding. Ask...Why am I here? Why did I choose it to be now?
You are aware that you sit at the Table of Life. All which happens on the Earth-Plane is governed from this Table. The choices were so important as to cause you to leave this table to enable the work to be done to be achieved.'

KEYPOINTS TP35
a) We all originate from the one GOD.
b) The present Time in mankind's History is of great significance.

6.57 'You have been given this lady, (Helana), to guide you. Your awareness is buried so deep at the present time. Once it is released, you will not stroll away, you will run forwards. It is all there ready to be found. The work to be done is indeed important, you are not fully aware of the extent of what is needed. Little by little you will understand. The work will be completed by the children you leave behind. It is all there, when their full potential is liberated. It takes many years to bring to them the compassion and direction, which they will need to find. You will teach your children. You will be a great Teacher. A gentler manner is necessary; this will come in time. Wise ways, true ways, will rise to the surface in you. This Lady is gentler. Your children will become Healers; the previous lessons were necessary to prepare these children. At no time will a trail of unhappiness be left behind.'

KEYPOINTS TP36
a) Your Mind can completely suppress your Spiritual Awareness; it can take much application, determination and Spiritual assistance; for the awareness to come to the fore.
b) All is planned; all experience has a purpose.

6.58 Jesus continues: 'allow your Mind to think in terms of a preparation, in order that you gain a fuller Understanding. There is no reason for you to feel guilt if you think in these terms. There is a grand Order of things, all our Lives are inter-dependent, and all are needed for any one Life to be complete and for the objectives to be gained. Helana has an understanding. You, John, should allow yourself the Time to gain an understanding also. We in Spirit have been surprised by Helana's knowledge; she has acquired this herself without any 'special help' from Spirit. It is her hard work alone, which has brought her to her current level of Awareness. You must quickly do the same, it is needed at this time.'

KEYPOINTS TP37
a) All Lives are inter-dependent for the experience to be gained.
b) It is possible by shear hard work to gain your Spiritual Awareness, if your will and application are there.

6.59 'Your complete Understanding of Northern Ireland will be gained in a short time. We see your Lives coming together and are pleased. Now, there remains only the question in your Mind of whether you will achieve the friendship and the strength that is needed within your relationship. It remains a mystery to your Mind as to why this is important, but Happiness is all-important within both your Mind and your Spirit. Your Spirit is in need of all the data for it to be able to rise. We can see within your eyes and Heart that the feelings for Helana are deep and true. However, more evidence needs to be available in your Mind, for your Spirit to see this. It is more than being together, it is a question of sharing a new Life, a new direction and a new outlook on your Life.'

KEYPOINTS TP38
a) Happiness plays a key role in our Lives and in the direction we follow.
b) Evidence of Love and true feelings, are seen in our eyes and in our Hearts.
c) The Mind acts as a doorway to the Spirit. The Spirit sees the thoughts, monitors the feelings, assesses the true affinities, before deciding on any reciprocal actions.
d) Your Spirit, in conjunction with your Spirit Guides, oversee and control the direction of your Life.

6.60 'You John, have an affinity with London; there is no such place in Ireland. Can you survive without this? There is very little entertainment within the places you will go, but you will meet many People. A clear Mind is needed. Habits will be abated. Speed is not necessary.

Blue skies are fewer, aggression is not needed. There are so many things that will be different. These are the questions you need to ask yourself in all honesty, upon your return to England. We will wait a few short days following your return, for you to come to terms with all that you see. We will give you time to find your true feelings. Allow your time spent in Ireland to be free. Listen to the people, enjoy your visit, we will leave you free to enjoy your time together.'

KEYPOINT TP39
All experience is for choices to be made, and for understanding to be gained. Time is allowed for the Mind to analyze and decide upon preferences.

6.61 'We understand your needs, to be with Helana and the child. But, more is needed, the Love has been found, but, the choices were made here, at the Table, to come to Earth to achieve at this Time. The work is needed. But, without your happiness also, the work cannot be achieved in the same Way. We understand your free-will to want this to be. We will allow this. It is to be if all else is settled in your Mind.

We do not expect miracles, but what we need to see is your conviction and compassion for the people of Ireland. That you feel within your Heart the help that is needed. The Love of your Life is to be second place at this Time. Your Relationship is safe. You need now to find a freedom from Love, to allow your Mind time to explore, and to question, and to find in your Mind what is needed. Peace and serenity will surround you both.... Go now in peace and allow this time to be free and happy. We know you have the strength to achieve this. Our love surrounds you at the present time and always.
Remain seated for a little while for the words to register deep within you. Understand this is also difficult for Helana, who also requires your Love.'

KEYPOINTS TP40
a) All Life has a purpose. It is planned before we are born.
b) There exists a controlling hierarchy of high Spirit.
c) If your motives and commitment are not correct, a greater purpose will not be allowed to continue.
d) Our Lives can be monitored and controlled from above.

6.62 We have planned our first trip to the Republic of Ireland, and on Sunday, 21st June, find ourselves staying overnight at The Park Hotel in Aintree, near Liverpool. On the Saturday, 20th we have attended the wedding Ceremony and celebration for my nephew, Timothy, which was held in Croydon, Surrey. Subsequently, we drove back home from London, and then up to Liverpool, by car, some 200 miles away. We intend to explore Ireland, and to return home on the Saturday of the 27th June. It was an uneventful, pleasant drive north on the Sunday morning. I have checked the prices and costs and have decided to drive my car, and to cross from Liverpool to Dublin (Dun Laoghaire), using the Packet Steam Ferry Company.

6.63 It is 22.00 hrs. we are staying overnight, waiting for the Ferry to leave on the Monday morning at 08.15 am. I am sitting on the bed, writing, when a message is delivered from Jesus: 'Your Lives can be heaven on Earth if you so choose. Every moment is special, and every moment demonstrates that you are part of Nature. Love yourself in all that you do. It is no good if there is distress or unrest in anything that you do. A release of anxiety in your Mind is necessary to allow you to begin. It is within your grasp, but a peaceful Mind is necessary.
We understand the Importance of your Journey, take care to know that we have your interests at Heart in all that you do. Our Love and Light surrounds you Both at all times'.
{We are excited and apprehensive about this 'leap' into the unknown, and worrying about being able to find the Ferry Terminal and to arrive to Board in time}.

KEYPOINT TP41
A quiet, peaceful Mind is essential, to be able to communicate clearly with Spirit.

6.64 'A strange place, a strange room; understand Helana, that all is well within and around you. I bring to you peace and Understanding. Do not be distressed in your Days together, you have a greatness of Mind and Spirit to achieve that which you must do, to enable the work for Spirit and for the World to continue. Your eyes have met, and your Spirits entwine to enable this work to continue. You have a greatness of Spirit and Mind my Dear, you have been chosen for this work. Do not put yourself down my Dear. We bring to you peace, to know that this will be. Your Mind will be sufficiently peaceful to enable your Spiritual Growth. Spare your Spirit the agonies of the Past, and allow yourself to move forwards. You have a charm, which only you can use. You will succeed. You were always intended to be the mother of this Child. The child needs a mother with a love so pure, and gentleness and loving nature, which cannot be found in many. Only you will see the beauty of this Time, No words can describe this.

KEYPOINTS TP42
a) Spirit bring peace and love to quieten your Mind and fears.
b) There is a greater Purpose to our visit to Ireland, which is beginning to emerge.

6.65 'John, in your Mind, your Spirit will rise, and you will see in Helana's Eyes the Mother and Lady of your life over many, many, Years. You ask of the Places to visit in Ireland. We have given many Places, these will suffice. Upon arrival you will have Time together, you may share this with Spirit if you wish. Work will begin the following Day…………………………………

Dublin is where you will begin, a more suitable Place to your needs will be found later. Your Sights will be set on Mountains and Greenery; these will bring about what it is necessary to see every Day of your Lives. A feeling of Euphoria will be found. This Land offers Warmth and Comfort and Beauty, which you have not previously found. You may share this with one Another, but also speak to the Child within Helana, and allow it to Know, and to Share in the Beauty. The Child is within, to Share and Grow with the knowledge of the Love everlasting, which you share. To Experience and to share all of the precious Moments which happen to you. Acknowledge the presence within of the Child. It is your Child John; you have been given the Seed to make the Child into so beautiful a Person in years to come. All is given, it remains now only to see, and to accept this Land.'

KEYPOINTS TP43
a) **Jesus is confirming that Helana is pregnant, that I am the Father, knowing that as far as I am concerned that I cannot father a Child, because of my Vasectomy.**
(Verified that year at Hospital that I had no sperm)
b) **A Child within a Mother is receptive to all Emotions and Feelings which the Mother displays.**
c) **Love is visible in the Eyes, Strength is a feature of the Spirit, and Compassion comes from your Heart.**

6.66 'The Child's homecoming is welcomed in Spirit. The Child will blossom, beautiful in Face, in Body, and in Mind. Do not speak of this, it is important. Many Others will wish to see this Child, it must be kept a secret. It must live a normal life, to avoid the Passions of Jealousy and Greed etc. which will arise in many People. We ask you John, do not reveal this to anyone other than Judith...You are a team of Three, a strong Band to fight the cause of TRUTH, HONESTY and SPIRITUALITY in its truest form.
I know, believe these Words, we will be with you to Guide and Help you. Allow your Mind to be Free, to see what there is to see...this is necessary in order to combat all the Forces of those in Opposition.'

KEYPOINTS TP44
a) **Should any Child be born who has special Gifts, How then, would it possible for a normal development without the pressures of Publicity in our Society today? If such a Child is born then it will need to happen outside of the public domain, if the normal Relationship lessons are to be learned.**
b) **Jesus refers to the war that is raged on the Earth-Plane between the forces of Light and Evil.**

6.67 'Helana will find that there are many Times when she cannot go on; but, the love of this Child will be with you. She will have a strength all of her own. She has promised to Spirit that she will not let go. Her love for the World enables us to see her true Strength and Character.
She may seem a little confused and silly at times, but she has a true Strength to pull you through; we have seen this Strength.
Bring to her John, the Knowledge that she needs...these words come with the true depth of feeling from my Heart...I walk besides you always. You have succeeded in friendship and a bond that will not be broken...this will enable you to carry-on with a greatness of Strength. Understand I am high Spirit and your Friend at all times. Allow us to Guide you; Go in Peace.
God places his Trust in us...We are one Family. We are true Friends.'

6.68 Helana is asked to read aloud Psalm 83

6.69 Jesus continues:
'Bring to these People of Earth the Knowledge of the one GOD.
Bring to these people of Earth the Knowledge of your Love.
Bring to these people of Earth the Knowledge of Sharing, and of Nature.
Allow them to see the Beauty of your Love
Let them understand the Purpose of your Life
Tell them about the Beauty that is around People at all times.
They do not See, They do not feel the Breeze; They do not understand the Rain.
Their Lives are filled with Pain and Suffering
Allow them to see the Beauty of all Things and Nature.
Do not let your Mind cloud your Judgement
It has to be your own Choice, your own Judgement.
We bring only the Knowledge and Hope that They, and You,
Will see the Beauty that surrounds you.
Go now, and let us know.'

6.70 Jesus brings the Knowledge that:
a) Mary, my Mother, is alive in the Land at the present Time. She will not be known to you until you return to Spirit'
b) IRELAND is the Heart of the World...Heal the Heart and then you can Heal the Body, {i.e. *the rest of the World*}. The rest will fall into place once Ireland is healed.

KEYPOINTS TP45
a) Affirmation that History is to repeat itself, that the current Time in Human History is very significant. That the souls from Biblical Times are gathering again for the new World.
b) The conflicts in Ireland are viewed as a cornerstone to solving ALL the problems throughout the World. The Heart needs to be healed and strong for the Body to be capable of being healed.

~~~~~~

7.09 We find lovely lodgings at Letterkenny and dine well in the Town. The Landlady's sister has become a Nun after an 'Psychic Experience' and a useful discussion follows.
At 23.00 hrs a message is received from Jesus...
'You have experienced all the Feelings of this Land, and its Emotions of Hate, Sadness, Despair, Warmth, Bleakness, Mountains and Fear. It has been a good Day, we are pleased. There is to be no turning back for either of you. You will share a Lifetime in this Land and bring forth the Child in this Land.

The Child is within, stirring, and will bring great joy to your Hearts. So much good and Understanding will come from this Time; there is now no separation between you. Dream not, for reality has become fact. You can see the Beauty of this Land, but what is lacking is Love and Understanding, there are so many who do not see. They see peace as only a means of materialistic Gain. They are in need of guidance and Understanding. To gain the respect of these People a friendly manner is essential. We have seen this. You shine so brightly amongst the darkness of their Minds. Amongst all the clutter and the devastation of their Lives, you have brought a ray of Sunshine. They wish to touch and share with you these Feelings. Your eyes will see so many things when you begin your work in this Land. You and John are as One, this message is for you both, you have a togetherness of a unique kind. At this time be aware of these steps, you will then see and hear many Things which will disturb you. Helana is aware of these Thoughts and feelings; they are necessary for her work. You need to understand the workings of your own Minds, so that you can appreciate other Peoples' views. You, John, must not try to possess Helana, allow her her Freedom, to do and to act as she chooses!'

7.10 'Do understand these Words come from Jesus, who walks beside you and cares so much for the Work ahead. I wish only to guide and help you, and not to enter your Lives. We understand the pressures are great upon you. We have given you a journey for you to enjoy and to see the sights; it has also been combined with lessons. We try our best to fulfill our needs with your own needs. Time is so short on the Earth-Plane. No definite plans have yet been made, because we needed first to be sure of your feelings. You will be shown again places to allow you to truly decide where your Heart lies, for both you and the Children. We understand isolation is not needed, but Peace, Water, Trees, Mountains, and Aspect are. You share the same views and feelings. There has been no disappointment, and no greed with what you have seen. A working together has been seen. Reach-out with both Hands and grasp what is on offer. You will be shown many places.
Togetherness has been found in every way, and we share with you everything. You have put the Past behind you...you have walked away and taken on-board the challenges. Now, open-up your Hearts and let Spirit in. Go in Peace, knowing we are beside you at all times.
Let your Hearts be filled with what you see. Take care to know that these words come from a true Friend who walks besides you.'

7.13 Whilst we stand on the Causeway Stones, (supposedly created by Nature), Helana receives a message from Jesus: 'Spirit was impressed by the perseverance of the Spiritual People who built the Causeway. They lived in Caves (now washed away), overlooking the Site. They believed that if they could build sufficient 'steps' from the Sea to the Horizon that they would be able to reach Heaven. The time was 18,000 years BC. These Peoples were not Humans in the current sense, but forefathers of your Race, John.'

KEYPOINT TFV8
Ancient Peoples (Aliens), who traveled to the Earth before modern Human Times commenced, constructed the Giant's Causeway.

7.14 On Friday, we visit St Patrick's Grave and the Cathedral at Temple Patrick. Messages are received from Jesus...
'We ask you John, to bring the Masonic Order into the 21st Century'
Whilst looking at the picture of St.John holding a Book, the Words are brought...
'You are more blessed if you give, rather than if you receive'
We stop at the Round Tower at Donaghmore and hear..........................
'Free the Minds of these People'
We pass on to Newcastle which we both like, but we then register the Hostility when driving over the Mountains of Mourne, on route back to Dublin, IRA flags and graffiti are evident everywhere.

7.16 Jesus states 'Sleep is needed to bring you both strength, as the peoples of this Land drain your Spirit, as they are so in need of Light. recognize these feelings, as they will help you with other people. John also has felt in a different manner. Working together, you will find it useful to understand the feelings of Others and to agree between you what is needed at a later time. We have asked you this day not to work for Spirit, but to understand the feelings so that once you live here, you will be able to immediately relate to the people.
Remember their history, they are blinkered. Their towns reflect this, in many Places you have felt sadness and tears. Understand the needs of these Peoples. You have been shown many beautiful things...Places, objects, colours, and trees. We hope that you have gained memories which are stored for future Years, so that you can look back and remember once your Life begins here. Already you have begun to fill in the gaps and crevices, which were filled with darkness and sadness and so in need of Life, Love and uplifting. Remember these times and experiences.'

KEYPOINTS TFV9
a) Thoughts do interfere with people's Lives; they are transferred into the Minds of people. When those people return to the Spirit-World, they will have gained an Understanding, which will help to change their situation for the Future.
b) Others can drain the energy from your Spirit. This can be re-charged when you are asleep and at rest.
c) High Spirit can take your Spirit away for healing, such that when you awake you may feel drained and exhausted, until your full Spirit is returned.

7.17 Spirit tell us that it has been difficult for them to communicate with us in this Land, as our sensitivity has been closed down to protect us. It is important that our Spirits are at the correct vibration to enable effective communication in the Future.

KEYPOINTS TFV10
a) The achievement of Spiritual Awareness, and the ability to be able to communicate with Spirit, is related to the level of vibration of your own Spirit.
b) Raising of our Spirits is therefore not only the raising of the physical position within our Bodies, but also an increase to their vibratory rate.

7.18 It is Friday 26th June; we have been directed by Spirit to avoid certain towns such as Attica, Hilltown, Newry, Dundalk, Drogheda and Belfast, as Spirit are protective towards us. I am told to expect a Spiritual surprise by Helana. We return to England via Liverpool. Spirit tell us that all that was needed has been achieved on this trip...
'Do not fear that a house is being prepared for you, and this will be shown to you on a future occasion.' My Guide comes to me for the first time through Helana. 'Helana is an instrument for Spirit as you are. Take Helana's ways as true ways. The writing you have done is not from your Guide. It is not possible at present for you to directly communicate... trust in Helana, and allow her the freedom to be your Guide. Have trust and faith in Spirit. Helana knows true Spirit. She is unhappy for your attitude and actions John are restricting her Awareness. You need to accept her as a more spiritual Person.
Your Spirit John will remain buried unless you let go of your Earthly Mind. Learn by the lessons that you have been given... you have so short a memory! Share your food with someone else in need, in this way you will not feel uncomfortable afterwards. Keep your Back straight; this will help with the communication. Do not worry about leaving food on your Plate, it is your choice.'

KEYPOINTS TFV11
a) Other Spirit can come to you and pretend to be your Spirit Guide; you need to find a Mentor to help you to avoid interference.
b) Your Mind is powerful enough to prevent your Spiritual growth. It is necessary for you to convince your Mind that you wish to pursue the route of Spiritual Awareness before real progress can be made. A straight Back helps to assist reception.
c) If when you eat, in your Mind you nourish others, you will not then feel so uncomfortable afterwards. Do not always eat food because it is there; stop when your Body tells you to.
d) Do not try to communicate with Spirit on a full Stomach, you need to feel comfortable, to be able to relax, and to 'switch-off' from the physical senses.

7.19 Jesus continues: 'Listen carefully to these words. Understand; do not think that it is fiction or tales. Read the book 'The World Unseen'. It takes a brave person and frightening experiences to be able to learn, and to progress, and to understand. Allow us to continue to bring the Knowledge to Helena, so that she can continue to grow. She can bring so much good to Others. Helana has expressed a wish to share her Life with you. Listen to her. Do not tell her what to do. Do not rule her Life. Allow her her freedom, it is Love she gives to you of a true kind. She is there in pureness of faith and spirit to enable you to grow your Spiritual Awareness. She has seen many Lives taken from her; she does not wish this to continue. She has the trust and faith that your Spirit will continue to be raised; to be at one with her is all that she wishes. Allow her this happiness to see your Spirit raised. She will not remember these words. All that she does is for your Spirit. Do remember this, Do read and re-read and remember these words.' *{it would seem that my Actions are still causing problems to Helana}*

KEYPOINTS TFV12
a) Jesus is confirming that High Spirit are assisting Helana's Awareness to grow. He also states quite clearly that one of Helana's purposes is to assist my Spiritual Awareness to grow.
b) It needs a brave Person, and some perhaps frightening experiences, for growth, learning, and understanding to take place.
c) It is necessary for my Spiritual Awareness to grow, in order that Helana's can grow, in order that I may grow. Our progress is linked as we are of the same Peer Group.

7.20 'Release the misery and pain of your past-Lives. Shake-off the guilt of your Past. Move forwards with your Heart, and your Spirit, and your Mind. Words alone are not enough. Do not doubt these words, I am of high Spirit. There are great works to achieve. Your work is precious for the people of this Land (Earth). It will be a sad day if the opportunity is not taken in this Lifetime. You have been given a Lady to love you, and to support you, Helana also has different work to do. This will continue with or without you. Your work John, will continue, and you will father another child, but Helana's Life will be shared with another, if you continue not to understand these words. This is not wished for, but Spirit need to see a greater commitment from you, not just words. Two people are ultimately better than one. We leave you now with peace in your Heart. Read these words often. Helana does her very, very best. You cause her so much pain. You do not realize that her life is a Spiritual one, she has a beautiful nature. You will learn so much from her, allow your Spirit to grow.

Take these words into your Heart. We are with you every moment of the day. It is the truth, it is not a fairy-tale!'

KEYPOINT TFV13
```
Simply saying that you wish for your Spiritual Awareness
to grow is not enough. You also need to clear the guilt
from the Past, and to commit with your Heart, with your
Spirit, and with your Mind.
```

7.22 'Be yourself, be that person with a raised Spirit. Let it be, care not what Others say, be they family, friends or people in the street. You are who you are! Believe in your allegiance, but first listen, live and breathe in Spirit and in the one GOD. The well-being of Helana's Spirit concerns High Spirit if she continues as she does now. Helana must be allowed to be more Spiritual. You must be careful what you say to her, and how you say it. Almost all of her decisions are made by Spirit. Helana has chosen to continue to help you against the wishes of her Spirit. She struggles because your Mind is so strong, but your short-term memory is so poor. Remember the times when your Spirit is raised. Aim for the skies, they are within your reach. Let our arms enfold you, you are in need. We wish you peace in your Mind and success. Allow it to happen.'

7.29 Jesus states: 'That which can be found on the Earth-plane is kept forever by the Spirit and is more valuable than lessons learned later in Spirit-World. The hurdles you experience on the Earth-plane are there so that you gain Knowledge, so that when returned to Spirit-World, High Spirit can learn from these lessons, and use them to help other Spirits............

Your Mind John, is strong so that the lessons can be learned, so that on your return these lessons can be used by Others. Remember, these days of learning are for the benefit of Others, as well as for your own Spirit. The knowledge will enable Others to progress more easily. Look upon these days, as days of hope for Others. If you succeed, you will bring to Others this hope. You have chosen this Life, so that you may gain all that is needed. You must examine and understand the purpose for your Life.'

KEYPOINTS TFV17

a) **There is a Purpose to Everyone's Life. When you achieve Spiritual Awareness, you will know what your true purpose is.**

b) **It is easier for the Soul to learn the Lessons needed on the Earth-Plane. The Lessons needed are presented to you, for you to learn. Every day and every event is there for you to Learn.**

~~~~~~

8.00 It is Sunday, 5th July, 1998, when we receive a message of encouragement from Samuel, Helana's Guide and also from Jesus. 'All is to happen as previously given. Your relationship has been tested and found to be satisfactory. Your awareness will now grow. We ask you to view the videos 'Highlander' and 'Abyss'. You need to find peace within your Minds and your Beings'

KEYPOINTS D1

a) **It is necessary for your relationship to be satisfactory, before the work and your awareness can develop.**

b) **Events and situations will be brought to you to test your relationships, your determination, and your commitment.**

c) **There are lessons to be learned from videos and the words within songs.**

8.05 Jesus states: 'You have earned this time together, and you should use this to repair the damage of the Past. You will gain a great deal of Understanding through your Time together. Many lives were lost by you in the Past when you stepped backwards; but now, even in your short Time together many steps forward have been taken. As Leaders of a Church a great deal of progress will be made. A strength has been found, which will carry you forwards, tripping only on small stones. Large ones can be overcome if a spring in the step can be found. You have both a great need and strength of Mind and character to prevail in all areas. Courage, tenacity, surefootedness will be with you both. What is needed will be found in your Hearts and Spirits...you will remain Together. We see the shear determination, courage and friendship, growing steadily and surely...like Trees in the ground, standing the test of Time, we feel sure the roots will hold you in place for many, many, Earth years. Every Step which you take in this Life brings you closer to healing the Past. You need to Soul-search and find reconciliation of your Past Lives; but; only refer to these memories at certain Times.'

KEYPOINTS D5
a) A Church is to be formed…. The Church of GOD on Earth.
b) It is possible, through the wrong choices, to fall backwards away from the Light. This has happened to us both in previous Lives.
c) It is possible to heal the Past, to ask for forgiveness, to stride forwards towards the Light and Love of GOD.

8.06 'Be aware, do not falter, do not stray. Do not take each other for granted, do not get lazy, for all can change at the blink of an eye. A moment's disturbance can upset a lifetime of Dreams. It has been given that a marriage in Spirit has taken place, understand the vows are held in great esteem, to be listened to and to be understood at all times. Care not what others may say. Forget your Past Lives, we see no return to your old ways. It is needed, it is asked for. Rebuild your Lives, strength and positive ways are called for. You both are to work alongside the highest realms in Spirit to bring this about. We have chosen wisely and believe it can be achieved. We have seen the determination in your Hearts to continue.

Step aside from the hurts of the Past. Dream only about your Future together. The treasures of the Earth can be found in your Hearts'.

KEYPOINTS D6
a) GOD holds marriage and the joining together of Souls in the greatest esteem.
b) A Hierarchy exists in the Spirit-World; there are Levels of purity, understanding and wisdom to which you can aspire. The seven Spiritual Levels of Achievement refer to this.

8.07 'The Skies rejoice in what they see. Bring sunshine into the Lives of Others so that they can see what can be achieved in their own Lives... A blessedness, a glory, a haven, a beauty, many, many words can describe what we hope will be achieved. Do not allow Others, or memories, to put aside the treasures that can be found in your Lives...See the light at the end of the tunnel. It can be seen. It can be reached. It is long, but it can be traveled quickly without faulting. But, remember my Dears, there is much to be seen along the way. The tunnel is lit by candles to show you the way. It is not dark, you will not be weary. You will travel the miles on many Backs who will carry you safely in times of need. Shoulders also will be present to bring to you strength and support. They are wide shoulders. Reach out also for the hands that guide you through the tunnel'.

KEYPOINTS D7
a) Spirits are there to help and support us on our Pathways through Life. We are never alone.
b) Always pray and ask for help and it will be brought to You. If YOU do not ASK, how can YOU hope to receive?

8.08 'Speak only of this my Dears to friends of a true Kind. Announcing to the World is not necessary, it will be read in the pages of a Book, which will be written. Allow your Children to see in the Lives of their Parents how great thou art...You have promised that you will continue to bring about this work for Spirit...Each one a different role. Your efforts are needed so much. You will be given the strength to continue this work. fear not, peace will reign; you will be guided. Take only that which is offered; no more, no less. Speech will come to others who are in need of guidance and trust. Go now in peace, and remember we are by your side in all that you do. Angels surround you as you work. Go in peace.'

KEYPOINTS D8
a) The writing of this Book has been predicted by Jesus, some two years earlier. Caution has been stressed throughout this time, the dilemma being, how much to tell those around us, without telling them too much, but hopefully enough to explain our actions as rational Human-Beings!

b) White Eagle has also predicted the writing of this Book in 'The Living Word of St John', and 'The Lightbringer', both written many years earlier and published by the White Eagle Publishing Trust'...see appendix.
c) We are reminded to take ONLY that which is necessary. And reminded NOT to fall into the trap of greed, possessions, and the material Life.
d) We are told and re-assured, that the strength, guidance and words necessary, will be brought to us to enable the work to proceed.
e) ANGELS exist and come to us in times of need. Many miraculous events, when Lives are saved are the consequence of Angelic intervention.
f) We all have a Guardian Angel, with us at all times on the Earth-Plane, it sometimes is possible to see your Angel if you wish to.
g) Angels are a separate Species, who work tirelessly for the one GOD. It is possible, by exception, for Humans to progress to become Angels. The Arch Angels direct and control the activities of the Angels.

~~~~~~

9.25 Jesus states 'She has even shared the burdens of my Life. It is for this reason we set aside a place in the highest of the Heavens, to bring to you both, the rewards that you deserve. We are delighted to see the coming together of these wonderful Spirits, we could not have chosen better.! We see you growing stronger and stronger by the minute. You are a powerful Force in the World, and will continue to be this one great Spirit throughout Eternity. Understand John, why it is so important for Helana to be in Ireland. It is a great act she does for this World. Sleep is now necessary for her Spirit to recuperate, and to be still. There will be many tears. Understand, this is because of her nature and feelings for other Peoples'.

KEYPOINTS AB21
a) It is possible for one Spirit to take on-board, to share, to help to resolve, the burdens of another, but only with the approval of High Spirit.
b) It is possible to make a bargain with GOD, if you are prepared to devote your present Earth-Life for the benefit of Others, then you can expect some advantage. some, perhaps deferment of Karma, in this Life-time.

{the bargain is normally with High Spirit, who act on behalf of GOD} ....BUT BEWARE IF YOU DEFAULT!
c) ALWAYS be extremely cautious of what you wish for.
d) The POWER arising from the twinning of Spirits is far greater than that from two separate Spirits.

~~~~~~

9.71 Jesus tells me that when he was in his mid-teens he knelt down and prayed to GOD, using the Words 'Heavenly Father take my Life, do with it as you will, I dedicate my Life to your service'...All followed from giving this commitment to GOD.

KEYPOINTS AB43
a) It is a pre-requisite for any person who wishes to serve GOD to be prepared to walk away from all of their Worldly possessions, be these material or personages of any kind.
b) The pathway to glory of the Soul is not an easy one, it will involve many hardships and many tears. But the rewards are everlasting and cannot be lightly undertaken.
c) Every Soul has a Purpose, every Soul has a role to play, be this for one minute Understanding to be gained. Remember all is pre-chosen, the parents, the events are created. The Mind will then decide whether or not to follow the pathway.
d) Many fall by the wayside, many are far too ambitious. It is far better to adopt a lower objective and to be successful in that achievement; than to target the skies and then to fail and have to face the ensuing consequences.
e) This is not a solitary choice which affects only you individually, remember you are part of a Peer-Group of Souls who all need to play their part if your objectives are to be achieved.
f) The achievement of Spiritual Awareness will enable you the individual to become aware of what purpose you the Soul has chosen for this Lifetime.

~~~~~~

10.13 Jesus writes: 'Only in healing was I different to any Others. It is not necessary for me to perform the act of Crucifixion again, but it is necessary for you John, to gain a complete Understanding. Helana's tears were for your Spirit and sadness for the World. You John, do not have to be alone in this World; you now have a Partner who will share your burdens, Your tears, Your fears and Your cries of anguish and pain. You John, are the only man the Spirit of this child has loved fully. You John, will never be more loved by another in the Universe. You are united in Understanding and Love throughout Eternity. The rings placed on your fingers will not be removed for all Eternity. As a man you do not realize this, but upon your return to Spirit all will be revealed. Helana has not fully recognized your Spirit in previous Lives. Think, ponder and surmise upon these words in the deepest way possible.!! In the years to come, you will realize the greatness of the Spirit within you now. The work to be done has been needed for so long.'

~~~~~~

13.48 Jesus writes...... 'Cry for the World, your Bonding must continue, move swiftly from moment to moment. Place the bad memories behind your Door. Nature moves on swiftly. If a tree is struck down, seeds fall, a new Life starts quickly. It is the way of Nature. To harbour anguish and pain causes suffering and pain; the World will then suffer. Follow the lead of Helana, John, you will progress, you have until the Millennium to gain your full Awareness, it will take you the full two years. Your Mind is still in Darkness, but your Spirit has the Light and the Light will overcome the Darkness..................

We get frustrated, but we wish only for you to succeed, you have progressed, so much has been asked of you in so short a time. We wish you well and bring to you these words of encouragement. You are at one with your Guides, the one Spirit. You are not aware of your Spirit's presence within Helana, keeping her safe. Likewise Helana is within you. You both share messages and Guides and Angels and friends. You are finally through the barriers which have kept you apart. Understand, what is given will be given; only a short time now before you will be free of all these dark influences. These are working times, difficult and long...you have done well to come through this with your togetherness as strong as we see., have no doubt you will succeed and overcome Darkness, and in so doing the Lives of many will be saved.................

We thank you, we bring you these discomforts only for your guidance and help. We care so deeply, do not be angry. We care for all creatures and all Humans, all are in need, it is essential for you to succeed. Allow us now to see you at peace, in the knowledge that you are protected completely. Do not fear, for you have all the Angels and Love of Heaven about you....

You are a Messenger of Light to this World, we will not allow you to be in danger...The pains will now drift away. There is no danger, no fear, We talk not with anger, for they know not what they do. Go in peace and allow us to guide you.'

~~~~~~

15.26 Jesus writes.... 'Allow your children, John, to Be. They are aware of their roles that they have chosen, they are needed, and they will be guided by true Spirit. Grant them their Freedom...Many, many times we have said Love can only be found in Freedom...They will progress, they will return, do not offer them material bribes.. They will see the distance...they will search for true Love and will realize it is with the Father, it is only the Spirit of Elsa which prevents them coming to you..................

[I am concerned that I am not seeing enough of my Children]
It is written....'Let the little Children come unto Me'...this Lady Helana has the same Love of the World and the Children as I did....All is Shared. All is Given...There are many obstacles to overcome before these words become a reality...*(a vision is given of a Child suckling)*......Look at the Child suckle!....Understand that it takes all kinds of Love to create a World,...All is unconditional Love. Allow Helana to do this, it will take nothing away from the Love between you two...It is the same intensity of Love to all Things and all Beings and all Life...Allow Helana to do this, the Child within needs to understand this, it is expected of Helana to give to the Child; so the Child can give to the World...

Helana and you John make a powerful Spirit for the Child, a Spirit of beauty so needed at the present time. Rest assured, all is as it should be. What is to be, will be. Each individual has their role to play. Whatever is needed in their Lifetime, is preparation to be able to bring Love and purity to the Earth-Plane'.

15.27 'Your Child Edwin is a beautiful Spirit, he needs to learn strength, and strength of Character to do the job necessary. He will gain so much education from being with Elsa...He will see and hear when danger is afoot and be capable of offering protection. Look at his Life and be proud. Let not the hurt enter your Heart, they agreed to become the future Generation. What better Lesson to learn to survive in the Environment in which they are placed. All is as it should be...There will be another Child.'

KEYPOINTS DP08
```
a) All experience is given for Learning.
b) You need to experience and to receive Love and to
Love yourself, before you are ready to give Love to
Others.
c) All Lives are Chosen in advance.
d) There are many kinds of Love, all are Important:
* Man-Woman * Parent-Child * the World * Friendship *
Relatives * Other Creations etc.
```

15.50 At 03.00hrs on the 27th, I am told that my Spirit was taken for a meeting with Jesus, just the two of us, with no-one else present...
'there is much to understand my Friend, it is difficult for you, without the ability, to know and to remember, this will come as time unfolds. I thank you for your words and all harmony is restored. Man's emotions are difficult at the best of times, and events of the past weeks have been very trying for you. I am pleased that you seem to have accepted the situation and your Spirit will come to terms with this in a short while. All is progressing now as was originally intended. You have a key role to play and we welcome your cooperation and your attitude. All help and support will be given to ease your pathway. Events are moving now quite quickly, this is necessary. Your Awareness will progress also so communication will be easier and more reliable. I will return in a few Days to continue our discussion and to offer my help and support....................'

15.51 Jesus asks me through Helana whether I am prepared to follow in his footsteps, and to take care of Helana and the child...I respond yes to both questions, adding only 'to the best of my ability'.

##

{this ends the messages received from Jesus up to March 1999. Subsequent messages will be published in a further Book which it is intended will follow the Publication of the Book of Truth and Knowledge. Planned for June 2001. Further details will be available from the Web-Site at a later date.
See.........www.cogoe.org.uk}

messages from MARY, the mother of JESUS

[Mary's words and indeed some also from Joseph, were significant in the early Days of my Relationship with Helana. Her Role is one of 'THE MOTHER' and she forms a close link to Helana.
Helana with the HOLY GHOST within is asked to fulfill the Role of 'a mother' to the Peoples of the World, in particular to those in the Whole of Ireland. The BOOK also tells that Helana is being groomed for a Virgin Birth.]

8.56 On Saturday, 8th August, 1998, a message is received from Mary, the Mother of Jesus. The original words were written by me in red pen, at the request of Mary. We are still living in Aylesbury, Bucks, England. The Text reads:

'Have you felt different today?

A pleasant Day felt by many in this Land. Look at the brightness of the Sun, the Moon, and the Stars! Your wishes to become loving to Others, will be returned in the next few Days. You will see a marked change in your daily routine. You may if you wish to, remain the same; but we feel you will welcome a more peaceful existence for your time in this Land. Swiftly you will move forwards and experience a different and enlightened way of living in the new World which is opening-up.

Ireland will bring peace of Mind to your daily living, and your sights will be set upon achieving that which is within you. A difficult time ahead will be remembered, but this is necessary to achieve a " tidying-up of loose ends" A step-back needs to be taken from your families and friends...this does not mean that you will lose them entirely. Ships that pass in the night can be seen with the lights full on. Nothing is missed, all will be seen.

They will remember in their Minds, what they have seen, and felt, in your presence. They will be remembered in your Minds. Many will fall by the wayside. This is not due to lack of care by yourselves, but by necessity. Extravagance of words is not needed.'

8.57 'A carefree style of Life will be attained in time, putting aside the time for work for Spirit...The lifestyle will be different. A peaceful existence. Ordinary days. Set aside also time for music and laughter. You have a need for these times. We see so clearly your dedication for Spirit and the work which lies ahead. We wish you well and success in what you wish to achieve. This is not all that we ask you to do. There is the need also to achieve many things on a personal basis. Rest assured, times will be allowed for these, it will not benefit Spirit if you do not have the time. Today was set aside, a comfortable existence, conscious of Spirit and aware. We do not wish to take up your whole day with Spiritual matters.

Your own Lives are needed, to be together as husband and wife, mother and child, these are important. You need your own time also, for the closeness of being together...It is a question of balance'.

KEYPOINTS D41

```
Work of an Earthly manner, Funds, space, and time will
be found for this venture. Once again the need also to
satisfy Earthly needs and relationships is stressed.
A Balance needs to be found, to complete the tasks for
Spirit, but also to lead the Human Life.
```

8.58 'Within the Home a nesting Period has begun. It is satisfactory but it is not complete. We understand it is temporary, and appreciate the need for a more permanent existence, a safe home is to be found. Safeguard this knowledge. Memories of this Land will not fade away, they will remain'.

8.59 'Your future is to be so profound, I cannot explain in words alone, your Lives will be guided accordingly. You will set aside a time and a place for Healing; Healing Hands; for the work are needed. A testing time has achieved the process of bringing you together. Your Hearts, your Souls, and your Minds, will share so much. We ask you to keep it within your Minds that a swift departure will be necessary.
We understand the need for a temporary residence, one will be found. You have shared this time here with us. We thank you. I come softly and gently, I do not wish to harm the confidence of this Child *(Helana)*. So much is shared my Dear in your Mind. I will come to you in times of need...there is a strong possibility this will remain a necessity.!
I praise your name, you are a brave and a beautiful Spirit. You have seen the need, you do not fully understand quite what there is to be. Do not be afraid, we are here at all times, to comfort you in your times of need, and bring to you the support to guide you safely'.

8.60 'A little of your future is known to me. I come to you as a Spirit that has an understanding and need to be close to you at times. To bring you gentleness, and to safeguard your Minds. An affinity is also felt within your child's Mind. See not the dangers of life in this Land. Believe in your Heart that you will be protected at all times. There is no danger for the child if this is to be. Faith in your Hearts my Dears will bring to you an understanding of what is needed. All will be revealed in time, to guide you along the way. I will leave you now in peace, and it remains only for me to say 'GOD be with you in all that is to be achieved'. I remain close to you at many times, comforting you, and stroking your brow. Do not fear this'.

8.61 'Safeguard these hands John, they are beautiful hands which safeguard the World, as do your hands as well!
{I am sitting, facing Helana, and holding both her hands} Allow these hands to touch your face from time to time, feel the love within. You cannot see, but believe me when I say that these Hands will do no harm to any living thing...Plant, Animal, or Creature. Those who touch these hands will be healed in a way of Love and Peace. Allow Others to come as necessary, you will lose nothing. A Love that is shared is one so powerful, there is nothing lost, but all is gained by sharing. Gifts of love are showered upon you both, to give you strength in your Hearts. Speak only these words in confidence with special Friends. Not many now, but, Many will understand in years to come'.

KEYPOINT D42
Much is to be gained by the sharing of Love, Knowledge, Understanding, Compassion, and the material benefits with Others. Give and you will receive, but give willingly, without expectation of reward.

8.62 'It is hoped that you will act as a father figure to RAJ.
{Raj is my lodger, just 21 years old, who is a management Trainee, locally at Rothmans}.
He is now in need of direction, of compassion, of companionship, of caring, of Love, and of confidence in himself. Cleanse his Mind of previous Religions. He needs to have courage and bravery in his Heart to go forwards. His Family respect his needs, they are a good Family. Raj is needed to spread the word in the new World. He has been chosen as a Helper. Give time to his cause'

KEYPOINTS D43
a) There is no evil in money and wealth in itself. It is
the pursuit of these assets, at the expense of Others which is wrong viz .Greed. How can it be right, for one person to have so much, whilst Others suffer and die through neglect? viz. the Biblical story of the 'Eye of a Needle'
b) Those who have much MUST use a significant portion of it for the common good, if they wish to be redeemed. Otherwise the wealth will be removed from them in subsequent Lives. Consider the following:
c) Raj's Grandfather is a case in point. He acquired much wealth through his own diligent work and effort. He has then used some of this money to establish Schools throughout India for those who are less well off. It is therefore acceptable to Spirit that he keeps the rest of his wealth.
d) In many of my previous Lives, I personally have had much wealth...for example as the Duke of Westminster. Spirit tell me that I did not use this wealth for the benefit of Others. In my present Life therefore, it is intended that I should experience being poor, so that I learn more compassion for Others.
e) A local man is destitute, and feeds himself often by eating turnips and vegetables he takes from the fields around Banbury, Oxon. It is 1998. I gave him a lift one day in my car. He claimed to be the Lord Syon, and that he owned much of the Queen's Estate.

f) We discussed this claim with a local Barrister, and I even wrote to the Heraldic Office in Edinburgh. He was dismissed as an eccentric. Spirit tell me that he was in fact the previous Lord Syon, but, because he abused his wealth, he must now suffer accordingly.

8.68 On Monday, 10th August, a message is received from Mary: 'Your work in Ireland is so important, it must come first before anything else! It will be completed by your children. The decision whether to give the special child will be made, and will be reviewed, time and time again when you are settled in Ireland. The child, a girl, has been given in Spirit and will await the final decision, as to whether she is to be born in this Lifetime, or in your next. Your need is heard and Spirit is aware and compassionate. Your sorrow John has been felt. Helana sees the girl in Vision, I am told that I will be able to do this when my vision has cleared.
(Helana has a heavy Period, her tummy starts to normalize, and the doctor says she needs Thyroid tablets for six months.) I feel many cobwebs around my face when I sit. My ears are becoming more sensitive, when I blink; I sense a running water effect! Later that evening, at around 23.00hrs, we are asked to step outside to look at the stars in the Sky. We see four Shooting Stars within two minutes, and are told the display is for us!

~~~~~~

15.04 The Virgin Mary writes: 'John, our son, go in peace and Love, knowing that the peace and Light, and all Love will surround you from now on;. Allow your eyes to look upon the World in a tender fashion, so that when you speak your message with your usual forcefulness, the tender look from your eyes will only serve to help those people understand in the way that is intended.
All is given for learning, but it is necessary also to show respect and humanity to all of GOD's Creation. Those who choose to ignore the harmony for their own selfish gain will bring the wroth of GOD and Nature upon themselves and upon those whom they profess to Love... GOD is merciful. GOD will allow them a further opportunity to change their ways;...this is reflected in your eyes, whilst the words may be hard and the retribution severe, there is always compassion and hope '.

~~~~~~

A1.23 On Saturday, 8th July 1998
Judith carries out a Spiritual Operation on Helana's Body... '...Keep an opening within your Day to send loving Thoughts to Ireland. 'Mary, the mother of Jesus writes... 'Do not my Dear mistake your message for any other than one person who shares a great deal of understanding for your Life. Do not doubt your feelings Helana, you are a very special person chosen for your work in the future. Let not Other's achievements cloud the work in any way that you are doing at the present time. Helana, go now to your rest with a peace of Mind and understanding.'

A1.24 'It is imperative Judith; that Helana understands the importance of not allowing herself to be abused by the Spirit of Others. There are many stray Spirits waiting to enter a willing Body, and so live the life they gave-up for what-so-ever reason. There are also the Spirits of the People living, these are not so strong as the Spirit of those who have passed, but they can be equally damaging. Helana is a very receptive Spirit; she has learned so much compassion, but for her own safety, and to remain on the Earth-Plane, for the time that she is needed, she must call on her Guide and Doorkeeper to protect her. She is now being given a Maori warrior as her Doorkeeper...these people were a very strong Spiritual Race, Helana MUST keep asking for protection.'

KEYPOINTS HS07
a) **Your Being is vulnerable to invasion from Dark Spirit**
b) **You can request a DOORKEEPER to block access to your Spirit.**
c) **You can request help also from your Guide, but you must also make it perfectly clear to any invading Spirit that they are not welcome and must leave at once.**

A1.25 'Do you not Understand my Dear, that when a Spirit within an Earthly-Being invites another Spirit in, we can do very little but to try to show the host-Spirit the dangers of this.   An understanding of the dangers of this is necessary...John could have gone through this Lifetime with no knowledge of any of this, and for this reason, it may come as a shock to discover that all Love of Spirit is coupled with the dangers of these Spirit who are in Darkness still...Is this not why we wish to fight for the survival and upliftment of the Planet Earth.?

KEYPOINTS HS08
a) **It is indeed a battle between Light and Dark Spirit on the Earth-Plane.**
b) **The Soul has free-will of choice, to choose between the Light and the Darkness.**
c) **Dark Spirits are attracted to Dark Spirits, Light to Light, to cross-sides is therefore more difficult.**

A1.26 It is of course made more difficult because Helana came from the darkened Side, and many Spirit recognize her Spirit as such. It is therefore Helana's duty to Spirit and to herself that she does not allow these Spirit to come too close. Please ponder these words fully, a day spent in the open air to do this would be well spent. Helana must learn to guard herself against all Low Spirit'.

KEYPOINTS HS09
a) Time spent in the open will help to clarify the Mind and reduce outside influences.
b) Dismiss Dark and negative Thoughts from your Mind, this will help to reduce outside influences.
c) Think Loving Thoughts to attract similar Spirits to you.
d) Pray and ask for help, support and guidance from GOD and other Light Spirits.

A1.27 'Be in no doubt Helana of the danger you were in, not your Earthly Body, but if a Spirit can be made so weak, it can be taken over by another Spirit if it so wishes. We ask you therefore to know yourself most fully so that you are aware the moment that another Spirit approaches...there are times when Love alone may not be strong enough to banish these Evil Spirits. We do not ask you to send hatred to these Spirit, but to be so firm that they are fully aware that their presence is not acceptable.'

KEYPOINT HS10
The Earthly Body can be invaded and possessed by DARK SPIRIT. If this happens IT IS ESSENTIAL TO SEEK PROFESSIONAL HELP AS QUICKLY AS POSSIBLE.

##

messages from GOD

{I have no doubts that the words given here were delivered by GOD. GOD after all is the Supreme Power who can take any form and can choose whether to communicate directly, or through the High Spirit who report to him (her, it, as gender is meaningless) }

{this first message is delivered a few weeks before John and Helana depart for Northern Ireland}

12.100 Later that Evening we join with Judith, who delivers the following message to us. This, it is said will be our 'Last Supper' together.

'From this evening everything changes, the time has now arrived. We see the dedication within John and Helana...their Hearts already reside in Ireland.
Continue with your Earthly plans, fear not when things do not seem to go as your Earthly plans. Now that you are working, all may not seem in your best interests, but on reflection they will be.
John will need to continue to grow in the Spirit, but we are pleased with his achievements thus far. We see he is prepared, and will have no hesitation in applying himself. The work will be strenuous, not necessarily physical, but Spiritual work. He does not always recognize when working with Spirit, but this will come.
Helana needs to settle her Spirit; it is with some trepidation she journeys to Ireland. She will manifest by her presence, beauty and Love.
We will not allow you to stumble or to fall, we hold your hand.
Settle your Mind on those you will be leaving, as they have no part in your new Life.
We have called the three of you together, so that you can celebrate the coming together of your Spirits. From this moment on, John and Helana will go forward, they will only be able to confer with Judith for a short time. It may seem difficult at times, but you will succeed and go on from strength to strength. This does not mean that all contact with your Teacher will end, this is definitely not the case, but understand that Judith, from this moment, her Spirit needs to set-out on a different path. There have been many struggles, but later this evening we will show her precisely where she is to be and with whom.
There is to be much casting-aside of Earthly Beings, She needs your Love to help her.
Now, John and Helana, you will need to be supportive, and she will need lots of uplift-ment and encouragement. She has to walk away from all that is in this House.
We rejoice for all of you, for you three; the Love will carry you on, and up to greater heights. There are no three other Beings with greater Love.'
'There are rivers to cross and mountains to climb.
Know all of these things in the name of Spirit, for neither of you will ever walk alone again. We wish not to talk of Babies at this point. They will arrive in their completeness when you have settled in Ireland. The body of Helana needs first to adjust and feel comfortable in the Land. We have placed you in a suitable position for this to happen rapidly. There may be times when you physically miss each other, but know that your Spirits will still communicate with each Other.

Look up to the Stars, each of you will do so. Follow your own personal Stars, and walk with Love and Light in your Hearts.
You have proved to be very brave in accepting the messages brought, there are Many who would have turned aside. We thank you.'
'Forget not the road will be stony at times. The Earth-Life was never intended to be easy, but you know it is far easier with Spirit alongside you.   Let Christmas joy surround you. This is a special message for today. Tomorrow matters will progress rapidly.
Know always that the Love and the Light flows in you and around you. Let all know around you, who you come in contact with, to realize and to see the beauty and Love around you.'

[Chapter 13. NORTHERN IRELAND THE BEGINNING, tells of our first month living in the Province, during which Period, John is under savage attack from Dark Spirit]

13.49 We are asked to walk down to the Promenade in Bangor, Northern Ireland, and Helana is asked to say prayers of healing for the Sea and all the Creatures within...
'Helana is a Creature of Nature; her words have healed the Sea and the Creatures within the Sea. The Sea needed her healing tonight, and the words spoken will protect you John in your future travels.
You are a leader on the Battlefield, do not criticize Helana for her sensitivity, or her ways...she is a very special person with work to do of a special kind...
The Sea, the Earth, the Trees, the Mountains, the Sun, and the Moon, these are all Forces of Good. The Spirit within this Being, Helana, is powerful, and strength is given to those in need.... Their Minds are filled with Thoughts of Love...there is no other on the Earth-Plane who can ask for this...
If you are in need John, call upon Helana's Spirit who has the strength of the Universe...this is a new found strength given to Helana...She is in need of the strength of all Things Living. She sends out a constant stream of Love to all People at all times.... there is nothing for you to fear John; the Spirit within is fortified. Understand the protection is within you at all times...The Lord Most High brings these Words to you...The Lord Most High is as Love and Caring...do not doubt these words.'

{I believe this refers to Helana having the Holy Ghost within her, this explains why our presence alone is sufficient to 'Lighten an Area' and to change Peoples perceptions and attitudes...it will also help to explain how the 'Recovery Work' can be achieved when the power of the Spirit is sufficiently strong}.

13.54 I am suffering from shoulder-blade and forearm pain...Helana delivers the following words, which are written in full...
'All Things are connected, the pain felt in your Body is due to many burdens you have carried with you for many Lifetimes. These burdens have been carried by this Lady for so long. It is now felt that you should feel what it is like to carry these pains for one Man for so long. We see the dedication to this cause as one for the World, for this Spirit was aware that if true and pure Love could be found with you, then there is hope for the World.
The history of your Spirit, John, was known to Helana; she knew how hard this would be to bring to you, a Tyrant, the Love necessary to help you to progress. With all the strength that the history of your Spirit has gained, in this Lifetime she will succeed...'

'You John have already gained so much, we see the dedication as One, at One with the Universe; for, as you progress and discover perfect Love, so will the World see that it can be achieved, with dedication, honesty, and purity of Thought.
As both of you give to each Other, eventually the World will progress as it should, it is difficult for you to understand completely at this time, but understand that as you grow together, so the Universe sees hope and promise of better times to be. ...
You are watched so closely by other Spirits and by GOD.
Do not fear, it is with interest and hope in our Hearts that you will succeed, for the child within will carry forward the honesty, the Lessons learned and the feeling of Love will grow in the child. The child learns deep within the mother's womb, surrounded by darkness, but so much Love is given by the Mother Earth, there is no doubt in our Hearts that this child will not succeed, for the dedication is so great....'

'This message comes to you from the Lord Most High, we offer you comfort and hope that you may see. You are guided fully and kept safe from harm, you do not deserve the onslaughts, but valuable lessons have been learnt on both sides, both Light and Dark...
Valuable Lessons for the future, so that you can cope.
You have coped extremely well considering the vicious attacks you have encountered by all Parties. It has now come to a conclusion.
The personal attacks will cease and your freedom will be found. In future years you will connect with darker Spirits of the World, they will be contained, but you will be able to help them to progress...'

'Personal pains will now cease, unless there is a Learning need; they will not be replaced by Others' pains; remember these times for future occasions.
There will be no more Witchcraft; this is viewed most gravely. All that has been given has been given. ...

Eradicate all Thoughts of this Person *(Elsa)* completely from your Mind, if you stumble upon a memory, place it immediately behind your door. cease communication; use writing to communicate with your Children. Do not accept personal contact with this Spirit, use reflectors of a strong kind...'

'We ask you to contact the people given for the meeting in December; a great deal can be achieved by these People. Allow us to guide you completely. We thank you for your time and help given to Helana, she is in need of a great deal of support. There are many feelings about her from the Past, and from this Land.
Understand also, her confusion, when something that has been gained...when a Life changes so dramatically, to have broken away part of that Life is like another Being to this child; Understand these feelings and the delicate nature of this child, so attached to the Earth-Plane, so completely at One with this World, that she feels the pain of each blade of grass which is walked on.'...

'As a Forest loses a Tree, the pain is felt; so when the Awareness is slightly diminished, it is as the Forest when it loses a Tree. We hope you will understand more fully in Time, knowing it is given in Love for the World...
Helana is of an understanding of why this is necessary for her Love of you and the World. We have brought to her today Love of a different kind for her to experience, for her Spirit is in need. Do not be jealous, there is no need, all who come to this Child are welcomed with Love. They are kept at a safe distance by her Guides, they who come are aware of this and respect this, they do not stay, they visit only.'

'This Child of Light will bring about peace in this World. Through her actions, her presence and her children, for there will be more than one child, at a later date. The child within is safe and well, and wishing now only for peace in the mother's Womb. This will be given.'...
Go now in peace and reflect upon these Words. Let our Love surround you both and protect you completely. All that has been given will be given, but not necessarily, as you would expect.................................
Remember that you are of the Light, you will succeed. You have the power of Love between you, which will conquer all Darkness. You have the Understanding within.
Allow your Spirits to rise and shine, like the Sun amongst the Peoples of this Earth-Plane. You are Loved. You are surrounded by the Light so beautiful. You are safe and protected at all Times.'

13.55 My Spirit Guide Ahizar writes; 'The message Helana has just delivered was given by GOD, and CAN BE, IS, AND WILL BE.

14.08 KEYPOINT N4

{High Spirit have asked for more commitment from John, they are not happy with his attitude towards Helana, John decides to consider all those aspects of his life in which he is prepared to subjugate his Choices to Spirit. He is asked to reflect upon his Expectations of Others, his Experiences of the Life to date, his Attitudes to Others, in particular Helana, and to Identify his new GOALS as he understands them for this Lifetime.}

<u>GOD interjects at this point and tells John, that there is no one greater Purpose or Goal for him to achieve than to prepare the World in readiness for the coming of the New Messiah.</u>

14.39 Helana delivers the following message from GOD:
'John and You, Helana, have different roles to fulfill, which will take you along different pathways, you will often be apart by many miles, but you will come together at the End...
Be careful John; still your Mind, to ensure your messages are correct. Slow down and concentrate on the moment...Allow yourself, to grow slowly and steadily with Understanding.
Things do not happen quickly, as in Nature it takes time for Things to happen.
Helana has been brought to you, to bring to you the Lessons necessary to allow your Understanding to grow and to continue...All the Knowledge that was to be given is now near an End.
Helana is to concentrate upon Nature and the children of the World...'

'You, John, are to set-up the Church, to bring together the Souls of the Past, and to prepare the World for the coming of the Messiah.'
Your Pathways were chosen in Spirit. It is hoped, and it is given.
You John, have the freedom to achieve what is necessary for you. It is necessary also for Helana to have her freedom, to enable her to achieve her needs.'

{These messages were transcribed by John, and delivered in Trance by the Mediums Judith and Helana, in the period between October and November 1998}

{On 14th January 1999, at 03.24am. I receive an electric shock through my Body: which awakens me from sleep, and I write the following words:}

'The World is beset with evil, and the time is now nigh when the Earth will react in a manner which will take many Souls. A cycle of Events is to begin when the Human-Race will be slimmed to enable the few who will continue on the Earth-plane to change their attitude. The process will continue until an Understanding is reached. Watch and behold.'

##

messages from PRINCESS DIANA

{Princess Diana and John Lennon both formed a close 'Spirit' Relationship with Helana when she was isolated within her second marriage. She was an avid reader and follower of Diana and also turned to the music of John Lennon, which in turn attracted his Spirit to her}.

6.43 On Monday, 15th June, 1998, Helena receives a message from Princess Diana.

'I am glad to see you, but sad of what could have been for me.
Helana's thoughts are welcomed for my children. I come with the strength that will be needed. Helana is to do work similar to that which I did.
It is so sad to see so much suffering on the Earth-Plane, it is so sad to see the suffering, so sad.
So many cruel Things happen to so many People.
There are so many in need of kindness, and of thought, and of Love, and of prayer. A little Love and tenderness, a Thought is all that is needed.
You John need to help also.
Helana and I have had similar Lives; parallel pathways, so much loneliness. We are close now and will remain so. I am pleased to see the Love between you. I have been asked to come this Day for decisions have been made'.

KEYPOINT TP24
Spirits of those departed can choose to come to you, but also they can be <u>asked to deliver messages</u> by High Spirit. This implies Instruction, Tuition, Order and Free-will in the Spirit-World. Princess Diana has been asked to bring the Message for her Spirit comes frequently to Helana and the Relationship is already well established.

6.44 'I bring a message also for you John, I see what is in both your Hearts. Do not miss this opportunity, your time together is so precious to you, but also to demonstrate to Others a Spiritual way of Life. It is so necessary for parents, for people and for Teachers to show the way.
I tried, but did they see? They blunder and think only of their selfish ways.
Do they see? Do they hear? Do they listen to other Peoples' needs?
It took me some time to see this and to break-away. I could not stay in a love-less Marriage.
My Children have suffered since, but they would have suffered more if I had not parted.
It is your thoughts that matter to them. Distance is nothing.
It is Spirit which counts. I give my Love to my Children, my Spirit is side-by-side with them.
I come to them.
Your Spirit's presence can be felt by your Children. They will be Aware little-by-little; their Spirits are raised by your presence.
Helana too has walked away from her boys. She has a Heart of Gold, it broke her Heart to leave them, but she has now recovered.
She can now reach-out in other ways.

You have been told by so many. Understand, your children have a whole Lifetime to find out what is needed in their Lives.'

'Do not fear, they will begin to show the look of Love in their eyes. Your child Edwin is special, he has a wealth of Knowledge in his Spirit; he will be a Guardian Angel to the new child. He will bring comfort and peace to your Heart, he will make a difference.
Open your eyes and your Heart to all that you can see. If you do not, not only will it be a loss to me and for my family, but also to the World. It is only a matter of time before your Mind is free. Let it be in this Lifetime, there is so much to be achieved.
I wish dearly within my Heart that you achieve this.'

KEYPOINTS TP25
a) There is little point in staying in a love-less relationship, for you may well block the opportunity of finding your true-Love. Your children sense your happiness, they <u>know</u> whether a situation is loving or not. It is often better to part to find new happiness for them to share in.
b) Your children must make their own Lives. Do not use them as a prop, or an excuse for your own actions!
c) The achievement of Freedom within your Mind and Soul is what is required. I have called this Spiritual Awareness, when full two-way Communication occurs between your Mind and your Soul.

~~~~~~

8.39 On Monday, 3rd August, a message is received from Princess Diana. She tells us that she can now come in Voice, in Spirit, and in Presence, but she is not yet fully healed. (Princess Diana was killed in a Car crash on August 31st.1997)
She brings a message of strength to us both. We are told that we can call upon her if we wish to...

'Do not fear the Past, these fears are now taken away, have confidence in Helana. She will become a great Medium. Shut the door on the Past. Jesus is keenly interested in the progress of the child.
John will share in the love of Trees and Nature that Helana aspires to. Save the tears of the Past until a later Time, when you can look back with true Clarity.
I bring to Helana a clarity of Vision and Understanding'.

KEYPOINT D29
It is possible to call upon the Spirits of those in Spirit-World to help us.

≈≈

A1.21 On 3rd July 1998..A Message from Princess Diana...

'There is a need for positive thinking at all times...You have given your Man a start in his Spiritual growth, it is now for him to grow, but also within this you need also to care for yourself...
We will guide you to whatever you need...take care to know the child needs this also, for learning has begun.
Happiness within the mother's Womb is felt my Dear and brings contentment to the child's well-being...Your time has come my Dear to bring the greatest Gift into this World, a Child filled with Love and all the beautiful ways of Nature that only his Mother will see...
Your Man's pain will disappear within the next few days, leaving him with an understanding that will remain with him for the rest of his years. Go forwards my Dear with Peace and Love...this Lifetime is there for your taking to succeed, my Dear.'
{this message was not seen by John until June 2000}

~~~~~~

##

messages from ISAIAH

[The Prophet Isaiah is little quoted in this Book, this is for two reasons. The one that whenever Isaiah is personally involved, the message is quite profound, but also whenever messages have been delivered and recorded, at his own request all record of these have subsequently been removed. Isaiah's role is one of a watchful Seer, who becomes involved only to reinforce the words from Others and to stress the importance of a particular action.

{(12.11), (A1.43) were both received in September 1998;
(14.59), (14.60) were received in November 1998.
(Keypoint SB33) was received in December 1998.]

12.11 'It is quite an experience to come in this manner.....It is so heavy here...How any of your Spirits can feel uplifted in this Earth Atmosphere I fail to see!
Know please, and understand the Importance of what we hope to achieve. I send you the blessing that each of you and those within your knowledge, who wish to see the Light, can be risen above this darkened Atmosphere. May the Light of the Lord Most High, truly penetrate the Atmosphere here, to bring all that is needed to Lighten this Planet once and for all...Isaiah'

A1.34 Isaiah writes... 'With love in my Heart and many tears in my eyes. I pray my Dears these tears will turn to joy for the coming years ahead of you will be difficult at times, but all can be achieved.
Watch, listen, and learn John, and probe your Mind many more times than you do at this present time. Allocate some time within your Day for this process. You need to Understand your Lady is weak, not of Heart but of energy. Allow her the rest that is needed throughout her day, with understanding in your Heart. A return to the Past will not be necessary, but learn by the mistakes of the Past.'

KEYPOINT HS11
a) You cannot expect to Progress and to achieve your full Awareness without Healing your Past, shaking-off the guilt of this Lifetime and LEARN:
- **TO LOVE YOURSELF ,**
- **TO KNOW YOURSELF and**
- **TO FORGIVE OTHERS.**

~~~~~~

[November 1998 is a difficult relationship time. Following the move to Northern Ireland, John has been attacked by Voodoo; Helana is being wrenched apart by jealousy and the attacks from Dark Spirits from her Past. Her relationship to the Spirit of the one known as Jack is a source of continual stress. Into this situation Spirit are not happy with the attitude or degree of compliance from John. The relationship between Helana and John is being torn apart!]

14.59 Isaiah brings these words: 'I am old and frail, I have not the voice to use through this Child, the hands are knurled with age.
I cannot speak through Helana in the way that I would wish to...these words are from an old friend and Spirit who has come to help you.... Do not hang onto the old ways. Let go and move forwards... Look back if you wish to gain the understanding.. Ask questions if you wish,'

14.60 'I do not wish to frighten or cause you pain, but this work is very important. Your Spirit will also gain healing from this work...The work done by Helana for your Spirit is almost at an end...the rest is for you to learn and to understand yourself....

We offer Helana the greatest of thanks, for without her help, completed with a greatness of compassion and Love, this work for Spirit could not have been achieved... I grow weak, it is time to leave this Earth-Plane, and this saddened Land.

How our Hearts reach out with Love for this Child, for she brings such Light to this Land. So long have we waited for this Time, at last it has arrived and we can begin to see the Lightness transform this Land into beauty...The mere presence of Helana makes this possible, her Love is so great. Do not at any time begin to feel there is no love for your Spirit...You will learn. One day it will all be revealed. We respect Helana's wishes for the sacrifice she has made for your Spirit to grow. Sacrifices must be made for the work to be achieved, it is necessary to lose before there can be a gain...Helana will not remember this Message'

[It seems that Helana has chosen not to continue to live with me]

KEYPOINTS N19

a) It is necessary to sacrifice in order for progress to be made. We must choose to walk away, to give of Ourselves, of our Love, of our Time, in order that we can grasp the new Lesson, the new Experience, the new Opportunity, and in so doing our Spirit will grow in Understanding

b) Our Memories can be 'blanked-out' by Spirit, should this be necessary.

~~~~~~

KEYPOINT SB33, (TD19)

a) The Earth-Plane Experience is a purely learning ground for you to take back to Spirit, that which you have learnt. The Earth-Plane is NOT the Life, it is the School! Quote from Isaiah on 26/12/98.

##

Authors comments

I hope that as a consequence of reading these words that you will wish to support the ideals and aspirations spoken of and setout in THE BOOK OF TRUTH and KNOWLEDGE. This publication I hope is to lead to a ground swell of Action in the coming years, to enable all to live together in LOVE, RESPECT and HARMONY.
Help please NOW, if only by purchasing the Book and Merchandise and publicizing the CHURCH.
The True purpose in the Future, is to improve peoples Attitudes, to each Other and to Nature; and to so prepare the People for the New Messiah,

NOT THIS TIME TO END IN CRUCIFIXION...............JOHN